THE GAME
OF ADVERSITY

8 PRACTICES TO TURN LIFE'S TOUGHEST MOMENTS
INTO YOUR GREATEST OPPORTUNITIES

NICK DINARDO

THE GAME OF ADVERSITY

*8 Practices to Turn Life's Toughest Moments
into Your Greatest Opportunities*

ISBN 978-1-6196133-1-7

FIRST EDITION

LIONCREST
PUBLISHING

*To all those who impose limits on themselves.
Don't settle for less than your worth. Learn and
grow everyday. You can achieve anything.*

All my love to Sarah.

Dad, miss you everyday.

CHAPTER 1

IT ALL STARTS WITH ADVERSITY

"Whoever fights monsters should see to it that in the process he does not become a monster. And if you gaze long enough into an abyss, the abyss will gaze back into you."

— FRIEDRICH NIETZSCHE

Every story begins with adversity. From the everyday quarrels of your next-door neighbor to the war tales of World War II veterans, every story, at its core, is defined by conflict. Every novel you read, every biography you crack open, every inspirational story you hear…whether you recognize it or not, adversity is the secret sauce that makes or breaks each story. Why? Because part of what makes us human and part of what connects us to the human experience is that, on a daily basis, we have to deal with our problems with as much deft as we possibly can. And these problems make us who we are. Like a sculptor chipping away at the marble, adversity is what chips and crafts us into who we are and what we become. And unlike what people might believe, adversity isn't some fickle thing that you can opt into or buy out of. No; it's something everyone has to deal with all the time. It's part of what makes us human...part of what makes us who we are.

It all started off as an experiment—an experiment to figure out exactly how we can become the best versions of ourselves. When I dove into the empirical research, what I found was that the science and psychology research from the past thirty years provided extensive evidence for what I believed to be true: Adversity crafts us into better men and better women unequivocally. What we know about brain plasticity, positive psychology, and neuroscience allows us to bring validity to ephemeral anecdotal evidence. And this is a good thing. This isn't just theory, and this isn't just another gospel preaching to the choir. This is the truth, and in this book, my goal is to blend storytelling; cold, hard research; and action for readers so that we can leverage adversity to our advantage. We'll learn about the different types of adversity, how to identify it, and how to learn from it. It's a journey and it's a process, but it's one that you'll be glad—as glad as I was—that you took.

In this book, I'll provide the framework and the tools to get the most out of any adversity, whether it is as mundane as taking out the trash or as game breaking as perfecting your three-pointer. I believe sports has an amazing ability to capture our imagination. Through playing, watching, and analyzing, the lessons we can learn and teach serve as an amazing microcosm of the lessons we can apply to life. I carefully chose sports as a vessel to demonstrate how successful athletes have consistently used adversity to achieve the ultimate performance. The goal is to apply the adversity lessons in this book to athletics but, most importantly, to our everyday lives. And with this framework, we'll not just look at adversity differently but also effectively mine the benefit out of each and every situation. Imagine if every problem wasn't just something to be solved but something that could actively benefit you? Well, you've come to the right place. That's what I'm here for, and that's exactly what I'll teach you. Plus, the principles in this book will not just make us better at handling adversity (though that is pretty great). The greatest benefit is that the ideas in this book will make all of us better athletes, better writers, better entrepreneurs, better parents, better husbands, better wives, better sons, better daughters, and, most importantly, better people.

What's unfortunate, though, is that, for many people, the concept of adversity isn't viewed as a good thing. Instead, it's viewed as a bad thing. We perceive challenges as being bad and as things to avoid. Yet, our perception isn't just wrong; it's culturally unglued. Just take a look at the dictionary definition of adversity: adverse fortune or fate; a condition marked by misfortune, calamity, or distress. And here's the next one: an adverse or unfortunate event or circumstance. Here are the synonyms: catastrophe, disaster, trouble, and misery. Culturally, our view of adversity is pretty narrow, and most of us would go out of our way to avoid it. But, to be frank, based on my anecdotal evidence and my research, a life without challenges is not only a life not worth living but also a life devoid of meaning.

Much of the perspective presented in this book is counterintuitive to what your parents, teachers, and guidance counselors taught you while you were growing up. In fact, depending on where you live, it's counterintuitive to the very culture you were raised in. The truth is that the American dream wasn't marketed to you through turmoil, struggle, and difficulty. It was marketed to you as bliss, glamour, and ecstasy. Hollywood, media, and television all did a great job of shaping how we saw the world growing up. But for our purposes, they also did a great job of misinforming us about the reality of our lives. Now, more than ever, is the time to take matters into our own hands. Whether it was the media, your parents, or the culture you were raised in, it's time to really and truly start thinking. Sure, what I'll present here might be seen by your grandmother as dangerous, but the thinking that I'll present in the rest of this book isn't just a way to live your life; in many cases, thinking in any other way is actively detrimental toward you. Whether we're diving into the ancient realms of Greek philosophy or taking a crack at the most recent psychological research (with fun terms such as post-traumatic growth and assumptive world theory), all the ideas in this book have been studied and empirically validated. And without the effort of the great writers, psychologists, and scientists whose fingerprints are gratefully scattered throughout these pages, we would never have uncovered the evidence that gives us the crucial agency to become better people. Without a doubt, from scientist to writer, journal publication to novel, and teacher to student, these are the best ideas to get you on the road to consistent and reliable self-improvement.

I'd be foolish to say that all adversity is the same. The reality is that just like people, adversity comes in different shades and textures. Not every challenge looks like a *Rocky* movie and has a heroic finish. Some adversity passes away in a day. You deal with a heated coworker. You're late for class. Your girlfriend won't text you back. And some adversity is simply terrible. You get into a car accident. Your wife passes away. War hits. That's simply bad luck, and it sucks. But whether morbid, awful, or minor, as woo-wah as it might sound, the best science and psychology out there tells us that we can benefit from the situation, even if it's as small as simply gaining a little bit more patience.

A forerunner in this space, Dr. Norman Rosenthal, pointed out in his own research that there were three specific types of adversity: bad luck, bad choices, and the hero's journey. Bad luck is straightforward. A car hits you and you're in the hospital. Yes, at no point did you have any influence on the incident, but it happened, and now you have to deal with it. (The good news is, if you're reading this book, there are specific strategies to help you turn any bad situation into a good one. Stay tuned.) Next: bad choices. What is a bad choice? It's any choice where you're the catalyst, and whether intentional or accidental, things turn out poorly. It could be minor. You were too busy binge-watching *Keeping Up with the Kardashians*, and hey, looks like you forgot your wife's anniversary! Or you could have forgotten to study the playbook for Friday's big game, and now your team comes up disastrously short.

According to Rosenthal, the third type of adversity deals with the hero's journey. Are you a *Star Wars* fan? What about the movie *Rocky*? Chances are you've experienced Campbell's monomyth through film, books, sports, and many other art forms. Whether it's a movie or your own personal development, there is an ebb and flow in life; it's a bare-bones pattern that's taken hold in both history and the arts that history produced. Whereas in a perfect world, you want to decrease bad luck (nearly impossible) and bad choices (possible but hard), you actually want to have an increase in the hero's journey.

What is the hero's journey? In Joseph Campbell's beautifully written book, *The Hero with a Thousand Faces*, he explains the hero's journey as a framework of storytelling that has repeated itself not just through novels, movies, and entertainment but in our own lives as well. When we, the heroes, fight against adversity during the pursuit of something noble—whether saving the princess or running up the seventy-two stone steps of the Philadelphia Museum of Art—that's the hero's journey. It's the golden standard for adversity, and it's the adversity that you—and you alone—seek out. If you're learning a language, that's the hero's journey. If you're reading a tough book, that's the hero's journey. Let's say you're terrified of heights. You don't want to be on a plane, you don't want to bungee jump, and you don't want to even see the sky right next to your window seat. Being able to look at this circumstance and say, "You know what? I should carefully test out whether or not I can overcome this and learn from this" is the better response.

Campbell, who was a huge fan of the novelist James Joyce, borrowed the term monomyth from *Finnegan's Wake* to better articulate the hero's journey. Campbell goes on to aptly describe the monomyth or hero's journey in his book:

"A hero ventures forth from the world of common day into a region of supernatural wonder; fabulous forces are there encountered and a decisive victory is won; the hero comes back from this mysterious adventure with the power to bestow boons on his fellow man."

The essential ingredient here is that the hero faces adversity in order to get something. And this is a framework that anyone can and should follow. Not good at water polo? Go practice and become amazing. Terrible public speaker? Go speak in front of an audience in class. Not fit enough? Buy a gym membership right now. It's the element of intentionality and the catharsis that gives the hero's journey its shape. Naturally, bad luck and bad choices spring up during the hero's journey. But bad luck and bad choices also serve, as you'll soon learn, as teachable moments. Looking and embarking on a quest to take problems and turn them over to your own benefit is what life, at its heroic and narrative best, is really all about. It's possible. It's doable. And it's up to you.

What's great about taking action isn't just that *life* propels you to action. Going beyond Rosenthal's work, I believe stories do too. Just think of a time when you watched a movie like *Glory Road* (a great basketball movie) and immediately had the urge to go drain a three-pointer. Or when you watched *Friday Night Lights* and just had to throw around the football. Just seeing the hero's journey in progress can add fuel to the fire. In fact, our greatest leaders used the stories and advice of the men and women before them to inspire them. Thomas Jefferson died with a copy of *Meditations*, a philosophical book by Roman emperor Marcus Aurelius, on his bed stand. Stories—whether a billion-dollar marketing campaign or a simple, self-published book—have the power to bring people to immediate action. As Alain de Botton, a British philosopher, puts it, books are a way of "saving time." We can live the lives of emperors, British imperialists, professional basketball players, presidents, and farmers, and we can travel the world—all by way of stories. We can better identify adversity and learn from it, almost skipping a step and hacking the system. In a way, it's beautiful. The narrative of someone else can inspire the narrative for you. It's the reason why the most successful people are enthralled by the arts, whether it's a book, film, or painting. It speaks to them. And more than anything, the arts provide a close examination of the human experience, and we relate. It makes us feel, and more importantly, it makes us move.

I've personally been inspired not only by the biographies of famous athletes but also by the athletes themselves. To be able to look at things and be touched, motivated, and have empathy for those situations...that can be a great source of personal power. And reading these stories can be an amazing way to go through the hero's journey at virtually no cost to you. An example: Bill Belichick. His grandparents emigrated from Czechoslovakia to pursue a better life for their family. But, more importantly, Steve, Bill's father, also started getting into football. And Bill, as a young boy, was privy to his father watching and analyzing game film. From a young age, Bill not only respected what his father did but also soon let what he did become the fuel for his passion. And this propelled him. In the very same way, Dr. Norman Rosenthal was able to meet Viktor Frankl, the internationally acclaimed bestselling author of *Man's Search for Meaning*. Here, Frankl recounts his experiences at Auschwitz—not only surviving it but, surprisingly, finding something to live for. Dr. Rosenthal noted how just meeting the man inspired him and his work for the rest of his life. And this happens all the time. Heroes inspire us, and they make us do things we wouldn't otherwise have done, because they're living proof that it's possible to do them. And, everyone (including me) wants to be a hero in their own way. There are people I have in my own life, people I know closely, and people I'll never meet who have changed my life.

Throughout the course of my life, my grandfather, Ben DiNardo, served as a tremendous source of inspiration. Just like Bill Belichick, my grandfather's family moved from Abruzzo, Italy to Western Pennsylvania, leaving what they knew behind to pursue better opportunities in the US. He was one of twelve kids, and his parents didn't have a lot of money. At a young age, he worked in the coal mines to help support his family. He went on to play football in high school and excelled. (Because of his thin frame and excellent speed, he was even nicknamed "Shoulder Pads & Pants" by his coaches and teammates). Then, World War II broke out. He folded his jersey, packed his bags, and went to war. He was one of many brave soldiers who stormed the beaches of Normandy. There was a particular moment, he recounted, when he was sitting in a U-boat with his fellow troops, playing cards. He remembered the feeling that maybe, just maybe, this was the day he was going to die. They were in their early twenties. The U-boat opened, and shots came guzzling in. My grandfather's story still inspires me. Whatever I go through, whatever I've done, I'll most likely never endure that kind of hardship or trial. But if I can look at that and be inspired, you have the opportunity to be inspired by the men and women in your life as well.

I'm writing this book because I have a responsibility. This responsibility is to share my hypothesis and research with you. I am writing this book for my past self both as a warning and as an opportunity to leverage the adversity that presents itself in our lives to our advantage. This is the most important set of lessons and research that I've ever encountered, and it's fundamental to everything I do. And that's why I'm writing it. The best part is that you don't need a PhD to learn this. As multifaceted as the ideas might be, they're pretty simple to implement. In this book, I'd like to unpack these ideas in greater depth and provide you with not only a framework and the tools to tackle adversity but also with stories to help propel you. I'm just a guy who's been through adversity, and I've spend a lot of time researching and thinking about it; now I'm distilling that wisdom down to a concise, actionable format. If you've paid attention this long, then you believe in the power of adversity. You are open-minded. You are willing to put in the work to listen, synthesize, and execute (or challenge) the stories and lessons in this book.

I'm excited to dig in with you. Let's get started, shall we?

CHAPTER 2

THE TRUTH ABOUT HANDLING HARD SITUATIONS

"And once the storm is over, you won't remember how you made it through, how you managed to survive. You won't even be sure, whether the storm is really over. But one thing is certain. When you come out of the storm, you won't be the same person who walked in. That's what this storm's all about."

— HARUKI MURAKAMI

In our culture today, most people don't think that adversity is a good thing. Anyone will tell you: Adversity is stress, trauma, pain, and anguish. Yet, no matter how ingrained these beliefs are in people and no matter how commonly we try to avoid adversity, we all look at it the wrong way because we've never been trained to look at it in a constructive way. People who go through adversity are better for it—plain and simple. And whether we look at the empirical evidence or we look at the anecdotal evidence, adversity can always be turned to our benefit. The adults in our lives might've preached the opposite. Every now and then, we believe that some hard things (especially "hard work") help us to get better. But beyond this adage, people don't, at their core, buy into how handling difficult situations can make us better. Instead, their beliefs find solace in comfort, luxury, and loftier ideals. And it's this baseline belief—the one that avoids adversity—that could not be more detrimental. Adversity isn't just good for us; it's necessary. To be happier, to be better people, and to lead greater lives, we desperately need adversity just like a dying man in a desert needs water.

And the empirical evidence confirms this. Martin Seligman's research with the US Army on post-traumatic growth is seminal in understanding why learning to handle adversity effectively is crucial. Seligman gained notoriety for his groundbreaking research on "learned helplessness," which decoded issues in helping people deal with depression. When people go through trauma, the general consensus used to be that they suffer—plain and simple. But Seligman had a different stance on the issue, and he believed people could use the trauma inflicted upon them to become even stronger. So, he started building a resilience program at the Univeristy of Pennsylvania, which developed a curriculum for teachers to understand how resilience worked and to teach it to the students. Now, Seligman has adapted the program for the US Army. The focus is on teaching soldiers the skills involved in developing resilience. The 40,000 drill sergeants go through a "train the trainer" program, and once they've mastered the curriculum, they go on to train the entire organization. The army has replicated the program, adapted it to address the lives of soldiers, and now teach the 40,000 drill sergeants who go on to train the troops. Both programs were a hit. Post-traumatic stress disorder, as challenged by Seligman, doesn't have to be the default reaction to extreme trauma. Instead, you can grow from it. Do you focus on trauma or growth? You have the agency to grow from your trauma, your pain, and your suffering. It's just a matter of getting the mind right.

In a recent study published in the *Journal of Personality and Social Psychology*, 2,400 people were asked questions about their own negative life experiences. What was surprising? Those who had gone through negative life events consistently reported better mental health and overall well-being than those who had not. And some of these negative life experiences were very real and very harrowing, from violence, social stress, and relationships to disasters and illness. But the study brought up an interesting question: If these people went through bad events, why were they happier? In the study, one of the most surprising findings was this: It's very possible to lead a terrible life having zero lifetime adversity, as illustrated by a U-shaped curve. If you don't go through adversity, you don't know how to handle it effectively *simply by virtue of experience*. In the study, this meant poor life satisfaction. The point? Living without adversity isn't ideal; in fact, it's actively bad for you. Zero adversity can derail anyone's life or even keep one from being on the rails entirely. The spoiled, awful, unhappy rich kid is a cliché for a reason.

Whether it's your happiness, success, or relationships, adversity is the constant in each one and is an inescapable truth. Your ability to deal with these points of adversity is proportional to how well you can foster each one. Handling adversity, and handling it well, is critical to channeling your experiences to your personal advantage (in fact, it is the single greatest source of personal advantage). The better you handle adversity, the better your life will be.

CHAPTER 3

NURTURE, NATURE, AND REALITY

"Needs are imposed by nature. Wants are sold by society."
— MOKOKOMA MOKHONOANA

Imagine this. We have identical twins: the same DNA, the same looks, the same insides. They were the same twins in high school whom you confused more than you'd like to admit and even now can barely tell apart. Now, let's take these twins and separate them at birth. As soon as they're born, they're reared in completely separate environments: different parents, different upbringings, different households, different...everything. They're the same people—the same twins with the same DNA—but are in wildly different environments. Now, let's take twins who were brought up together in the same household as a control group and compare the two sets of twins. Here's the surprise: This was an actual experiment that took place nearly thirty years ago, and its implications are far-reaching.

The researchers had a few questions: How will these two sets of twins turn out? How will this go? And what does this say about nature versus nurture? It was about figuring out how much of who we are is ingrained at birth and how much of who we are is a function of our environment. Interesting things started happening immediately. First, some of the identical twins in the same household actually ended up being wildly different. Yeah, they were competing in the same household, yet they took on very different roles within it. On the other hand, there were twins who had never met who also ended up different as well. The research is by no means conclusive on whether or not we're 100% nature or 100% nurture. But, as Martin Seligman states in his book *Learned Optimism*, around 50% of a person is genetic, and the remaining percent can be learned through experience, explanatory style, and growth mind-set. And this is good news. Controlling all the variables, especially all the variables of someone's life, is a near impossible task. But the science is clear: Who we are is a combination of nature versus nurture. It's all contextual, and we have the power to change it. If it wasn't—if we didn't have a choice—would I have written this book?

Yes, there are things that give you a specific predisposition to maintaining a growth mind-set and being self-aware. But your environment essentially does the same things: Over time, it cultivates these traits within you. The interesting thing is this: It's not one or the other. Nature feeds into nurture, which feeds into nature. It all works together as a group effort, and by the end, who you are is a collection of the events that happen to you. You are the end result. By intentionally putting yourself in environments that are difficult and challenging and by understanding yourself on the hero's journey, you override nature and build your inner greatness—but only if you are equipped with the right tools to flip adversity into advantage.

Some of the progressive research has come from leaders in the field of neuroplasticity (brain plasticity)—Norman Doidge and Michael Merzenich, the authors of the books *The Brain that Changes Itself* and *Soft Wired*. Prior to the 1970s, the consensus among scientists was that the human brain was relatively fixed—or hardwired—after a critical point in early childhood. Most forms of brain damage and mind-sets were seen as irreversible, and the attitude was nearly apathetic. But over the last thirty-five to forty years, significant research has proven that the brain is far from fixed. Instead, it is supple, plastic, and regenerative, even for those in old age. The process is straightforward: As the brain takes in new information, it rewires itself and forms new neural connections that change the matter of the brain itself. The key point here is, of course, that the inputs matter. Whether you're a voracious reader or a dedicated gym goer, you are kneading the flour that is your neural network. And this is liberating. What you're doing this afternoon has a neural impact on who you are going forward, however small, however big. As Robert Greene argues in his book Mastery, "People get the mind and quality of brain that they deserve through their actions in life. Despite the popularity of genetic explanations for our behavior, recent discoveries in neuroscience are overturning long-held beliefs that the brain is genetically hardwired. Scientists are demonstrating the degree to which the brain is actually quite plastic—how our thoughts determine our mental landscape. They are exploring the relationship of willpower to physiology, how profoundly the mind can affect our health and functionality. It is possible that more and more will be discovered about how deeply we create the various patterns of our lives through certain mental operations—how we are truly responsible for so much of what happens to us."

THE STORY OF LOUIS ZAMPERINI

Growing up, Louis Zamperini was a privileged kid. He grew up in an affluent middle-class household, and his parents were great to him. He was born in a place where people were simply "raised right." And yet Zamperini was the cliché of spoiled and entitled. He was constantly yelling, smoking, drinking, and getting into trouble at an incredibly young age. And to add to his problems, he was involved with the wrong people. Growing up in a great neighborhood and a great community, Zamperini, through the slack of middle-class suburban living, brought most of his childhood misery upon himself.

In 1931, Louis got into trouble (again) but this time, it was enough for the principal to act: Louis was now ineligible for all athletics and social activities. Louis, of course, never joined anything and was apathetic. But his brother Pete wasn't, and he didn't want to see his brother fall by the wayside. At sixteen, Pete pleaded Louis' case to the principal. He explained that, even if it didn't seem like it, Louis craved attention. Maybe if he did something positive and received the praise he lacked growing up, he argued, it might be enough to change him. When the principal wouldn't budge, Pete asked him if he could really live with allowing Louis to fail. For a sixteen-year-old, it was a ballsy move. But Pete was a rare kid, and he was the kind of kid who could pull it off. In 1932, Louis was made eligible for athletics. And after a nudge from his brother,

Louis joined track. Soon, he started winning—a lot.

Meet after meet, something in Louis' mind changed. He heard all these people cheering for him. For Louis, it was a visceral experience. People were talking about him not as a joke or a reckless teenager but in pure admiration. "It was the recognition," Zamperini says. "Nobody in school, except for a few of my buddies, knew my name before I started running. Then, as I started winning races, other kids called me by name. Pete told me I had to quit drinking and smoking if I wanted to do well, and that I had to run, run, run. I decided that summer to go all out. Overnight I became fanatical. I wouldn't even have a milkshake."

Being in the local paper, Louis could barely believe his eyes as his track career started to take off. Within four years, the sport transformed him, and Zamperini became a world-class track star. At eighteen years old, he set a national mark for the 1500 meters. At nineteen, he ended up making the team for the 5000 rather than the 1500 and did so after only a few races. He went to Berlin and competed in the Olympics with Jesse Owens, and while he didn't medal, he still went out with a fantastic finish. Louis even impressed Hitler, who called him up, touched his hand, and simply stated, "The kid with the fast finish." Soon thereafter, Zamperini gained national exposure as the next upcoming great American athlete for the 1940 Olympics. Things, Louis thought, were finally going well.

But the turmoil of the 1940s eventually caught up: World War II broke, and the Japan Olympics were cancelled. As international tensions rose, Zamperini, on a whim, enlisted in the army and was deployed to the Pacific Island of Funafuti as a bombardier, but he was soon transferred to Hawaii to await reassignment. And then things for Zamperini quickly went wrong. On May 27, 1943, while aboard a defective bomber conducting a search for lost crew members, the plane malfunctioned and crashed into the ocean 850 miles south of Oahu, killing eight of the eleven passengers. Now, stranded in the middle of the Pacific Ocean with only six candy bars and a raft, the crew quickly entered into a fight for their lives. With little food and fickle rainwater, the crew used the remains of two albatrosses to bait small fish, all while fending off deadly shark attacks, nearly-capsizing storms, and constant strafing from passerby Japanese bombers. After thirty-three strenuous days at sea, McNamara, one of the three last surviving passengers, died. After forty-seven days adrift in the empty and vast stretches of the Pacific Ocean, Zamperini and Phillips finally crash-landed onto the Marshall Islands, only to realize they'd stumbled upon a Japanese fighting post. They were immediately captured as POWs and were held in captivity, beaten, and mistreated until the war came to a close in August 1945.

On July 2, 2014, Louis Zamperini passed away at ninety-seven years old, but not before he became the subject of two autobiographies, a 2014 movie directed by Angelina Jolie, and a pristine example for millions across the US. What makes Zamperini so unique is that with each moment of adversity— from the lorn, lost tale of a kid on the wrong side of the law to a fight for his life under the provision of the brutal and unforgiving Japanese Navy—Louis always doubted himself. And this is normal. But it was his resilience and his focus on transcending the pain that made him stronger. Despite a cozy, suburban background that could have made Zamperini soft and ill-fated, it ironically became a springboard that made Louis the man he grew up to become.

CHAPTER 4

THE ADVERSITY PYRAMID

"The most fulfilling human projects appeared inseparable from a degree of torment, the sources of our greatest joys lying awkwardly close to those of our greatest pains...

Why? Because no one is able to produce a great work of art without experience, nor achieve a worldly position immediately, nor be a great lover at the first attempt; and in the interval between initial failure and subsequent success, in the gap between who we wish one day to be and who we are at present, must come pain, anxiety, envy and humiliation. We suffer because we cannot spontaneously master the ingredients of fulfillment."

— ALAIN DE BOTTON

If you want to handle adversity well, you have to cultivate the right skills. Through experience, stories, and research, I've been able to boil things down to a few concise lessons that'll help anyone—really…anyone—to handle adversity well. The truth is that millions of people have used these techniques to craft better lives for themselves and the people around them; so it's to your advantage to use them. As I've stressed, the tools to craft your life are out there whether they are silently embedded in the actions of an athlete or explicitly written in the autobiography of a president. It is up to you and you alone to make the most of it. In the upcoming chapters, I'll walk you through all eight of these building blocks, and by the end of this book, you'll have the ammunition to take control of adversity instead of letting it control you. Here are my eight building blocks that'll help anyone handle adversity well. These are the foundational building blocks that'll help you develop a skillset for adversity and build an attack plan to grow from it.

MIND-SET

Mind-set is the cornerstone—the keystone habit—to using adversity to your advantage. Mind-set allows you the mental flexibility to find the seeds of growth within the (badly packaged) fruit. Mind-set is the first step—and the most important one—in getting everything right. Your mind sets you up for action. The right mind-set is the infrastructure for sustainable growth through adversity. Without it, we are approaching struggle like a house of cards: Success can happen, but over time, it won't last.

You can find the best case for mind-set in Carol Dweck's research. Dweck, a professor of psychology at Stanford University, had a simple question: Why did some kids crash

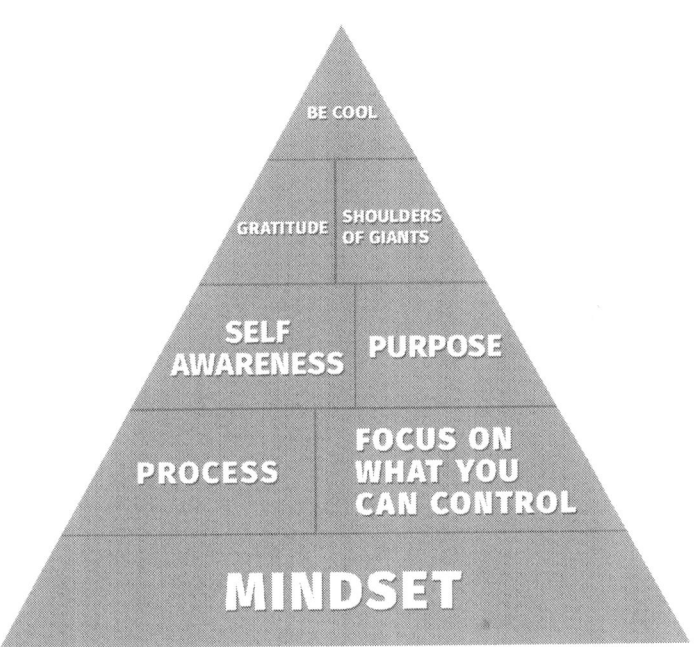

and burn in response to failure when others embraced it and thrived? Her evidence suggested that students who responded negatively to failure believed they just weren't meant to succeed at the challenge. Students who responded positively believed that the failure was a learning moment: an opportunity to understand what caused the failure and how to improve for the next try. Consequently, it was the beliefs that the students held about their intelligence that informed how well they actually did—more so than their intelligence alone. Some students felt that their intelligence was a fixed constant. Others rightfully believed that their intelligence had room to grow.

What Dweck carefully clarified was that there were two distinct mind-sets that set students apart—a fixed mind-set and a growth mind-set—and the research was conclusive: A growth mind-set was seminal in facilitating personal growth, while a fixed mind-set hindered potential. The students with a fixed mind-set didn't believe they could do better. Each failure was devastating and demoralizing. And for learners, this becomes a problem. On the other hand, a growth mind-set actively encourages students to enjoy challenges and seek improvement. This research reveals an amazing opportunity for us as human beings. In the face of failure, challenge, and adversity, a growth mind-set gives us the ability to build and act on resilience. We can build mental strength to break through walls in pursuit of what excites us.

If you were lucky enough to grow up in an environment in which you cultivated a growth mind-set, then you likely practiced persistence and valued ongoing learning, and you likely saw the success and fulfillment that others didn't. But what if you didn't? The most powerful aspect of Dweck's research proves that if you do not have a growth mind-set, you can develop one through targeted work and training.

PROCESS VS. OUTCOME

If you've mastered mind-set, then an understanding of the process is a natural by-product. By really knowing and understanding the process, we can take advantage of "human compound interest." Just like compound interest, our learning effort explodes over time. In the book *Money*, Tony Robbins explains an old gambler's trick on the golf course: "The gambler tells his mark, 'You play golf? I just started playing, and I'm no good. You want to play ten cents a hole?' So the guy says, 'Sure, great!' On the way to the first hole, the gambler says, 'You know, ten cents is kind of boring. Just to make it more fun, why don't we just double the bet every hole?' The first hole is 10 cents, the second hole is 20 cents, the third hole is 40. By the time they get to the fifth hole, it's $1.60. The sixth hole is $3.20, and they're only one-third of the way through 18 holes. By the time they get to the 18th hole, how much are they playing for? How about $13,107!" Every step, win or lose, is a learning experience in itself, and soon, when you reach the proverbial 18th hole, your dividends explode. That's the power of the process.

FOCUS ON WHAT YOU CAN CONTROL

There are so many things that philosophy can teach us. Two thousand years ago, a practical philosophy called Stoicism gained relevance due to its reliance on our human sense of control. Philosophers and leaders such as Seneca and Marcus Aurelius pioneered Stoicism as what Tim Ferriss would call an "operating system for living one's life." It teaches, amongst other things, that there are many events that happen to us. If we treat these as distractions rather than as things we need to respond to, we can focus on what we can control, leading us to more fulfilling, productive lives. There are so many things that are simply out of your hands. Your coworker is angry with her spouse. A car hits your mailbox. You lose the soccer game even though you tried your best. It might've happened, but guess what? It's also time to move on and focus on the variables you can control.

Poker players are good not because they have the best hands but because they know how to play the shitty ones. Whether the adversity comes from bad luck or the hero's journey, keep yourself in check and ask yourself this: "What can I control in this circumstance?" Is there anything you could change that could improve it? Are there things that you may be dwelling on—that you're just naturally holding onto—that you should really just mentally put aside? Because if you can't control it, the answer is to stop worrying about it and start thinking about your response. When you focus on what you can control rather than expending useless energy on the things you can't, you'll notice that life starts opening up for you.

SELF-AWARENESS

Self-awareness is a sense of knowing who you are, what

you're doing, and how this all fits into the complicated chaos of your life. Depending on our self-awareness, we adjust how and where we improve our circumstances. Based on our self-awareness, we apply a narrative about what life really is and how we should go about it. It's important to nail this. Martin Seligman's research in *Learned Optimism* cautions us against being self-critical. I believe that it is healthy. With anything you do, there's always a line, and when striving for self-awareness, it's one you'll have to tread carefully without straying too far into either melancholic self-judgment or hysterical self-delusion. This balancing act is, nevertheless, important.

CLARITY OF PURPOSE

It's not just about focusing on how much money you can make or how many cars you can buy. It's about focusing on a higher purpose…a higher mission—something larger than yourself. In positive psychology—more notably, in Seligman's research—the good life, the pleasant life, and the full life are all very much available options. But the full life offers the most: It's the life in which you have the pleasures, the engagement, the purpose, and the mission. Focus on the goals that are bigger than you are, while also channeling your efforts closer to a higher purpose, and you'll reap the benefits.

BE GRATEFUL

Appreciating adversity at its core is about putting the elements of your life into context. It's about unveiling perspective, showing gratitude, and understanding. From the war-torn, snowy pastorals of the American Revolution to the penniless New Yorker arguments of your grandparents, from big to small, and thousands of years to just now, all the lives around us have been defined by struggle. After billions of micro and macro decisions, world events, conversations, and moments, somehow, the end result was you. Appreciate the magnitude of your moment here on Earth as an irrefutable by-product of the historical human response to adversity. With perspective, we can remove ourselves from snap judgments, from getting too high or too low on ourselves, and become grateful for the work put in before us. From your friends to your coworkers, adversity touches everyone you know. As much as you want to avoid it, it's better to meditate in its wake rather than be held in its grip.

STANDING ON THE SHOULDERS OF GIANTS

Isaac Newton was praised for his brilliance in mathematics and physics. Yet he appreciated the contributions of the people who had come before him, when he famously said, "If I have been able to see further, it is by standing on the shoulders of giants." If you see other people doing something, you know that you can too—and even surpass them.

There is much to learn from the past. History provides us an opportunity to learn from achievement and failure, from joy and loss, from beauty and sacrifice. While we must face adversity, in various forms, each day of our lives... through books, film and other media we can learn from high performers in the fields we enjoy, and apply those lessons to our lives. These lessons can be sourced from the people we admire throughout history, and we can also glean much from research into our own family origins.

You are surrounded by a supporting cast of thousands, all of whom can help you through adversity, by providing inspiration, being a positive role model, providing emotional support—whatever it is, you're not doing it alone, and you know it's possible, because you're standing on the shoulders of giants.

BE COOL

Training is authority. As obvious as it may seem, preparation is really at the center of doing anything well. You prepare, you do well, and you're cool. You don't prepare, and it's a disaster. Being cool is a direct function of being prepared, but it's not just about learning your playbook or memorizing your formulas. We can learn to be cool in the face of adversity if we treat it like we do a sporting event. If we treat adversity with the right preparation, we give ourselves the opportunity to better deal with it under pressure. When we prepare, we can keep a cool head under pressure because we've already tasted the pressure. We can reduce our stress levels, make a decision that actually makes sense, stay calm, and stay cool. And this is optimal for performance.

CHAPTER 5

THE GROWTH MIND-SET

"And the day came when the risk to remain tight in a bud was more painful than the risk it took to blossom."

— ANAÏS NIN

In 1979, Bill Walsh took over what one sportswriter claimed at the time was the worst franchise in the NFL. For the San Francisco 49ers, conditions were bleak. It was Walsh's first professional head-coaching job, and at 2–14, the 49ers had one of the worst records in the league. With a disappointing management team at the helm, they'd given up their first-round pick prior to Walsh being hired. Conditions were dire, feelings were tense, the fans were uninspired, and the season and the future were uncertain. By 1988, however, Walsh was able to bring three Vince Lombardi trophies home from the Super Bowl and set the 49ers up for success for the next twelve years. In every word, they became a dynasty—a cornerstone of the league—and Bill's life changed forever.

It all started from humble beginnings. Walsh's father was a blue-collar laborer from Southern California—a hard man with whom Bill never built a strong relationship. Walsh, in spite of his candid communication skills, never really had many friends growing up. Growing up and playing football wasn't glamorous either. He went on to play football at the College of San Mateo and San Jose State. Walsh eventually took a coaching job with Marv Levy's staff at the University of California, Berkeley, but his credentials capped him. Walsh wanted to work in the NFL, but the odds were against him. Pedigree was held in high regard within the "good ol' boy" circles of the NFL, and Walsh's experience at San Mateo and San Jose put him behind the eight ball. Throughout his coaching career, Walsh constantly dealt with disappointment and judgment, with many people assuming he wasn't smart enough to understand football or capable enough to influence a team.

To overcome this, Walsh refined his ability to become detail oriented. Walsh, cultivating his own creativity and counterintuitive thinking, and he orchestrated more and more plays as if he were on the field himself. He knew exactly what the eleven people on the offense were doing. And once he was able to diagnose what the defense was about to do (a side effect of watching countless hours of film), he used his foundational knowledge and creative prowess to create new plays based specifically on the weaknesses of the defense.

Even when Walsh was starting out, it was clear he wanted to become a head coach. But as he started to work with Paul Brown and the Cincinnati Bengals, Walsh wasn't seeing the momentum in his career he had expected. Despite a stellar track record, the NFL calls he had hoped for simply weren't coming in. He later understood that Paul Brown had sabo-taged him. Brown had led owners to believe that Bill had no interest in becoming a head coach. Brown knew how valuable Walsh was, and he didn't want him to leave. So, he lied.

In 1976, Walsh left the Bengals to become the offensive coordinator for the San Diego Chargers. During the fol-lowing off-season, Stanford University called Walsh about a head-coaching job. When Walsh approached San Diego head coach Tommy Prothro about the opportunity, he told him frankly, "You have to take advantage of the opportunity... Good luck, Bill." Walsh learned a lot during his years on the gridiron, but Tommy's goodwill had inspired him: Walsh made it a personal rule to never, ever get in the way of some-one else's future. Walsh had already felt the sharp end of that sword in Cincinnati, and it wasn't a sword he had any interest in swinging.

Walsh's eventual success with the 49ers wasn't an accident. For Walsh, it started with a coaching style that emphasized mental preparation and attention to detail. *How you do every-thing*, he believed, *is how you do anything*. Now, more than ever, he made it a personal mission to get the players to approach everything with the same grace and deft he practiced. From tying their shoelaces to executing on the football field, the goal was to get the players to think about everything through a winning mind-set.

Throughout his career, Walsh developed another strategy that defined the 49ers: the West Coast Offense. Back while he was working for the Cincinnati Bengals as the offensive coordinator, his starting quarterback was Virgil Carter. Carter was a mobile, accurate passer with short to mid-range passes, but he wasn't accurate downfield. So, Walsh designed an offense that leveraged Carter's strengths and hid his weaknesses. The West Coast Offense boasted a horizontal passing attack with short, quick throws and used the running game as a complement. Like Billy Beane of the Oakland Athletics, Walsh was forced to build his strategy not on common football trope but around his team's constraints. Walsh's offense relied on timing.

After a 2–14 first season as the head coach and general manager of the 49ers, Walsh saw an opportunity. To pick his team up, Walsh told his players not the worry about the wins but to just focus on mind-set. With that, the West Coast Offense was refined until Bill Walsh had not only mastered it but had found the perfect weapon to execute it: the legendary quarterback Joe Montana. With an arm for short passes and an ability to move around the pocket, Montana fit the part like a glove. Over the next season, they gradually started losing by smaller margins. With Montana at the helm and a renowned sense of confidence, the second season proved more fruitful—6-10. Now they were starting to believe in themselves. After three seasons with Bill Walsh as head coach, the 49ers won their first Super Bowl.

Through all the rejection in his life, from his weak relationship with his father to his struggles as a young offensive coordinator, Walsh adapted. And it was because of these challenges—not in spite of them—that Walsh became one of the best coaches in NFL history. Later in his life, Walsh cowrote a book with Steve Jamison, as Walsh was dying of leukemia, entitled *The Score Takes Care of Itself*. Walsh opens the book with "I would never write anything that suggests the path to success is a continuum of positive, even euphoric, experiences. That if you do all the right things, everything will work out. Frequently it doesn't, often you crash and burn. This is part and parcel of pursuing very ambitious goals." Walsh recognized that his career was never a testimony of play after successful play. With so much competition yearning to tear Walsh apart, it was clear that it would never be.

"Pursuing your ambitions," Walsh writes, "especially those of any magnitude, can be grueling and hazardous, and proves agonizing failure along the way. For achieving those goals is among life's most gratifying and thrilling experiences. The ability to survive and overcome the former to attain the latter is a fundamental difference between winners and losers." In Walsh's coaching career, there were sixteen tenets that defined his own coaching methodology called the "Standard of Performance" (shown on next page).

If these ideas can help lead a sports organization to a multitude of championships, they can help you. Walsh's sixteen rules served as a framework for his entire business. These ideas spread not through memorization but through consistent action. From the secretary at the front desk to the star quarterback of the team, everyone was expected to live up to Walsh's standards. If someone had an appointment, they were to be treated with the same respect that a GM would receive. For Walsh, people weren't centerpieces; the organization was.

1. EXHIBIT A FEROCIOUS AND INTELLIGENTLY APPLIED WORK ETHIC DIRECTED AT CONTINUAL IMPROVEMENT
2. DEMONSTRATE RESPECT FOR EACH PERSON IN THE ORGANIZATION AND THE WORK HE OR SHE DOES
3. BE DEEPLY COMMITTED TO LEARNING AND TEACHING
4. BE FAIR
5. DEMONSTRATE CHARACTER
6. HONOR THE DIRECT CONNECTION BETWEEN DETAILS AND IMPROVEMENT AND RELENTLESSLY SEEK THE LATTER
7. SHOW SELF-CONTROL, ESPECIALLY WHERE IT COUNTS MOST—UNDER PRESSURE
8. DEMONSTRATE AND PRIZE LOYALTY
9. USE POSITIVE LANGUAGE AND HAVE A POSITIVE ATTITUDE
10. TAKE PRIDE IN MY EFFORT SEPARATE FROM THE RESULT OF THAT EFFORT
11. FOCUS ON WHAT WE CAN CONTROL AND BE WILLING TO GO THE EXTRA DISTANCE
12. DEAL APPROPRIATELY WITH VICTORY, DEFEAT, ADULATION, AND HUMILIATION ("DON'T GET TOO CRAZY WITH VICTORY NOR DYSFUNCTIONAL WITH LOSS")
13. PROMOTE INTERNAL COMMUNICATION AS BOTH OPEN AND ASSOCIATIVE, AND SEEK POISE IN MYSELF AND THOSE I LEAD
14. PUT THE TEAM'S WELFARE AND PRIORITIES AHEAD OF MY OWN
15. MAINTAIN AN ONGOING LEVEL OF CONCENTRATION AND FOCUS THAT IS ABNORMALLY HIGH
16. MAKE SACRIFICE AND COMMITMENT THE ORGANIZATION'S TRADEMARK.

THE GROWTH MIND-SET

Even today, Dr. Carol Dweck studies and develops the idea of growth mind-set and why it matters. Early on in her research, Dweck focused on how children responded to challenges. Her goal was to understand why some children shut down in the face of failure and why others thrived. What was the difference that defined them? After extensive research, she found the difference.

Initially, the research focused on the math scores of adolescents. Before she administered the tests, Dweck had specific criteria to determine whether or not a student exhibited a growth or fixed mind-set. What she saw was that students who had a growth mind-set consistently outperformed those who didn't. When the students with fixed mind-sets were challenged, they disengaged from the learning process. At a fundamental level, they didn't believe they were good enough. But the students with a growth mind-set thought differently. When they received a dip in grades, they perked up: "I'll figure out why I failed and do better next time." And this made all the difference.

More tests were run, but this time on premed students. Typically, premed programs are extremely difficult. A steel backbone and profound resilience are almost requirements. Yet, when students focused on praise that highlighted natural ability rather than work ethic, they underperformed. And when they focused on their grades, it was the same. This was found across the board.

Another research segment related to students' responses to errors. Dweck's research team measured the brain activity of students with a fixed mind-set and students with a growth mind-set. A 2011 study led by colleagues Mosier and Schrauder discovered that growth mind-sets produced intense brain activity: Students reacted to errors constructively and with more mental energy to craft solutions.

Imagine a picture of two brains. When they don't react, the color is blue. Now, with growth mind-set subjects, you see a rainbow of colors, indicating mental stimulation and healthy activity. But with the fixed mind-set subjects, there was virtually no response to the error, and in short, the screen was blue. It was as if the brain had desensitized itself to the error and learned to be helpless. With a fixed mind-set, the brain stopped functioning at a complex level. Prior to the 1970s, the theory that your brain evolved over time was laughed at by the best neuroscientists of the decade. The popular theory was that once you reached early childhood, your brain developed into what it would be for the rest of your life. Modern research has proved this theory to be false.

The key to cultivating a growth mind-set and setting the brain on the right track is the difference between ability praise and process praise: Ability praise—that is, "You're so smart!"—and process praise—that is, "You made a fantastic effort here. You worked hard at that." Salman Khan, founder of internationally renowned education platform Khan Academy, abides by Dweck's research and, accordingly, never tells his son that he's smart. Instead, he focuses on process praise: "Dad, aren't you glad how I struggled with that word?" his five-year-old son says. Through process praise, we promote a growth mind-set. Process praise focuses on effort and work ethic, which are under our control. Ability praise cultivates a fixed mind-set because the focus is on ingrained abilities rather than development and learning. This makes all the difference.

According to Dr. Carol Dweck, there are four phases to changing your mind-set from fixed to growth:

1. Learn to hear your fixed mind-set "voice"
2. Recognize that you have a choice
3. Talk back to it with a growth mind-set "voice"
4. Take the growth mind-set action

In this exercise, let's focus on getting step one right. This ability to identify your inner voice and catch yourself is critical to giving yourself the opportunity to change this voice. If we can develop this habit, the other three phases become much easier to implement.

EXERCISE #1

FINDING YOUR FIXED MIND-SET "VOICE"

What does a fixed mind-set thought sound like? Thoughts such as "What if you fail?", "You'll be a failure," and "It's not my fault; it's someone else's" are fixed mind-set questions and statements. The goal is to achieve consistency. With time, you'll be able to develop the ability to catch yourself during a fixed mind-set thought, reset, and apply a growth mind-set perspective. Here is an exercise to identify your fixed mind-set voice: **RECORD YOURSELF FOR A DAY.**

- This may sound extreme. However, think about if you were trying to improve your finances. Your accountant or financial advisor would tell you to record your expenses over the course of a day, week, or even a month. By performing this exercise, you are providing an unbiased record of all activities—some that you would remember anecdotally and others you wouldn't believe you spent money on. Doing this inventory with your self-talk provides a sometimes scary but accurate look at how you respond to events during a day in the life.

- Every hour, put together a minute-long recording of the events of that hour and your feelings.
- Work to be honest with yourself. Some hours may not include anything exceptional, but building the habit consists of doing the task consistently.
- When you have a moment at the end of the day or in the morning, listen to your recordings. Try to identify fixed mind-set and growth mind-set "voices."
- Then, ask yourself, "How can I improve this reaction?"
- Write it down.
- If you are serious, repeat this for twenty-one days.

Even if you do this exercise for a day, the goal is to start to develop an awareness of what your "voice" is. This provides us the opportunity to revise this inner voice with growth mind-set thoughts, which then turn into positive actions. Over time, you'll hone this muscle, which becomes the foundation of approaching adversity when it shows itself.

CHAPTER 6

THE SANCTITY OF PROCESS

"If the path be beautiful, let us not ask where it leads."
                                    — ANATOLE FRANCE

It's the 1998 Olympic Winter Games in Nagano, and eighteen-year-old Michelle Kwan is the favorite to win the individual women's gold. She's skated her entire life and for the '98 games, she's prepared. Mentally, her game is on point. Physically, her skating is impeccable. She knows her routine just as well as she knows how to breathe. For six minutes, the world's eyes are focused on her. It is skating at its best. Kwan and Tara Lipinski, a skater who had beaten her years ago, wait respectively for the final verdict. And the news comes swiftly: Kwan has lost.

Kwan grew up as the daughter of blue-collar Chinese immigrants. For most Olympians, it wasn't unusual to find parents forcing their kids into the sport at an early age. For

Kwan, though, it was the opposite. Even as a kid, her parents gave her the agency. Ice time cost only $5.75, and her father provided some options: "You can either use this [money] for ice time, or you can use this and go to the liquor store and buy candy." Kwan chose to use the money for ice time. As a young girl, it was a lesson she took to heart. This willingness to sacrifice short-term enjoyment for long-term reward would provide Kwan the opportunity to be the most decorated figure skater in United States history.

Years later, Kwan was to compete in the Olympics. Despite Kwan's impeccable 1998 performance, Tara Lipinski won. While second place would have proved devastating for many Olympians, Michelle Kwan reacted to the loss in a stoic, stand-up fashion. She respected her colleague, Tara Lipinski (also a US figure skater), and celebrated the win. Make no doubt: Kwan would've preferred the number one spot, but with two winners on board, the US brought home more medals, and Kwan respected that. When asked what it felt like to not win the gold medal, she swiftly responded, "I didn't look at it that way; I looked at it as 'I won the silver.'"

RESPECTING THE PROCESS

Michelle Kwan, now recognized as one of the most influential figure skaters of all time, respected the process. Even as a little kid, paying $5.75 each day to buy ice time was respect paid to the process. Kwan is the most decorated figure skater in the history of the sport, earning nine national titles and five world titles. In the 2002 Olympics, Kwan fell and received a bronze medal. When a reporter asked mid-interview whether she was in the Olympics to win it, Kwan quickly corrected her: "No, I stayed in to *try* and win the Olympics." It wasn't the end goal that mattered; it was trying that did. It was the drip-drip-drip process of constantly learning and constantly improving that mattered to her. She didn't look at her world as a series of outcomes. Instead, she looked at it as all part of a process. As Bill Walsh would say, when you have the process down, "the score takes care of itself."

Whether you're improving your social skills or figure skating in the Olympics, the process is critical. It's about enjoying the ride without the blinders on rather than worrying about the wins and losses. Some people say, "If I don't reach this milestone, I'll fail." But this line of thinking is not only poisonous but also unsustainable; when adversity is a reality, you have to plan for it. So be present in the process. Then, let the outcome take care of itself.

But let's dig a little deeper: Why exactly is forgetting the outcome important? I'll explain. Let's say your end goal is buying a dream house. Maybe it's a 4,000-square-foot colonial in New England with a well-trimmed, green backyard and a two-car garage. For most people, this feels overwhelming... even overwhelming to the point where they freeze—a classic case of paralysis by analysis. Instead, by breaking up this large task into small, achievable chunks, you don't become overwhelmed. You relax. You respect the process not by scrambling to get the big thing done but by doing the little things right and watching them add up to something great. Small wins give you the confidence to keep going, to keep growing, and to get yourself closer to where you want to go.

EXERCISE #2

A practical application to help anyone to start respecting the process is deconstruction, which is something I learned straight from Tim Ferriss and his book *The 4-Hour Chef*. The act of deconstruction can be applied to nearly anything. Ferriss suggests breaking down goals into "minimum learnable units," which are the building blocks that consist of whatever discipline one is focused on learning. Say, for example, you want to become a 9 handicap in golf, which is a lofty goal for some—me included. Now, break it down into its essence:

- Goal: to become a 9 handicap.
- What does this mean? It means that you have to shoot about an 81 over 18 holes of golf consistently.
- What is your current handicap? Let's say it's 90. This means you'll need to improve nine strokes per eighteen holes.
- What does improvement consist of per hole? To get from tee to hole, you need to practice these aspects of the game:
    - → Driving
    - → Fairway/Rough
    - → Approach
    - → Chipping
    - → Putting

What is the 20% of the work that would give us 80% of the results? Many golf experts say that the most important aspects of scoring is around and on the green. In fact, if we have ninety strokes in a round, around 40%–50% of these strokes are from fifty yards and in. Where should we focus then? Probably on chipping and putting. From there, it becomes a meta-process: understanding and respecting the process in the process you've identified.

Apply deconstruction to a new or existing discipline you want to learn or become better at. Write down each step of the discipline, and identify the 20% of the activities that will yield 80% of the results. This approach will help you understand the importance of process and bring a focus to the work ahead.

CHAPTER 7

THE POWER OF CONTROL

"To be in hell is to drift; to be in heaven is to steer."
— GEORGE BERNARD SHAW

On September 4, 1993, Jim Abbott of the New York Yankees was up against one of baseball's best hitters—Carlos Baerga of the Cleveland Indians—in the ninth inning. The scene was set—Yankee Stadium. He was one out away from a no-hitter, and no one had reached second base. They reached the count of two balls and one strike, and Abbott threw a fastball down the middle that Baerga could have creamed. But instead, Baerga hit the ball right to the Yankees shortstop, Randy Velarde, who threw it to first baseman Don Mattingly for the final out, giving Jim Abbott a no-hitter. The Yankees won the game 4–0. As of 2014, there have been only 239 no-hitters in Major League Baseball history. Yet, what makes this no-hitter unique is that Jim Abbott was born with no right hand.

Growing up in Flint, Michigan, Jim Abbott looked at his father as a hero. After every game, Abbott's dad treated it as a learning moment. If Jim had nine walks in a game, his father would give him a hefty lecture on dealing with failure. If Jim had a one-hitter at a ball game, his father would be there to talk about the importance of humility. But, what makes his relationship with his parents so important is that growing up, he developed the belief that he could do anything. Sound familiar? It should. This is the essence of the growth mindset—the belief that failure is a part of improvement and that learning is growth. No matter what happened, no matter what adversity Jim went through, he believed he could do anything. And this made a difference.

During his adolescence, Jim seldom acknowledged his deformity. But he did do his best to live with it, and his support system, especially his parents, helped him feel as worthy as the other kids did. During football season, the head coach needed a backup quarterback. During Jim's senior year of high school, he called up Abbott to play the role, even though Abbott had never played football in his life, and with no right arm, no less. But the coach won him over, and Jim joined the team.

So they focused on figuring out a way that Jim would play. They deconstructed the mechanics of the game. They focused on mastering the plays and perfecting the throws. And they focused on perfecting a style that would help Abbott play football effectively. Eventually, Abbott ended up not only snatching playing time but also leading his team far into the state tournament that year—a high school dream for anyone.

But if football was a hobby, baseball was his passion. With a ninety-mile-per-hour fastball senior year, the scouts were impressed. And the more he played, the less they worried about his right hand and the more they worried about whether or not he was ready to play professionally. After graduating from the University of Michigan, Abbott became the eighth pick in the 1988 draft. And soon, in the Major Leagues and in the '88 Olympics, he was able to play professional baseball and was able to play it well. With a formulated style that he could call his own, he thrived in the MLB. And eventually, after a successful ten-year career in baseball, he went on to marry, have two daughters, and become a motivational speaker.

FOCUSING ON WHAT YOU CAN CONTROL

We are all faced with constraints, whether social, racial, or socioeconomic. For Abbott, his constraint was physical. In one of Abbott's speeches, he made the point that "When something is taken away once, it's given back twice." With the constant switching of his pitching glove during each play, it became such a swift, practiced, and concerted effort that Abbott became as quick as anybody with two hands. Despite the constraint, Abbot focused on what he could control. He planned, he improvised, and eventually, he won.

Much of the groundwork Abbott operates from originated from the great philosophers Marcus Aurelius, Epictetus, and Seneca, who pioneered a practical branch of philosophy called Stoicism. Stoicism posits that focusing on what we cannot control is a destructive emotion and that the healthier, more productive strategy is to focus on what we can control. And the philosophers were right. Wasting our mental energy on things we can't influence distracts our mind from thoughts and actions that can benefit us and others. Here is an example: Say you did poorly on a math test. You can't go back in time and change the grade. So what can you do? Amass as many resources going forward as you possibly can to make sure you do better next time. You can only be your best self in this moment, because the past is gone. In the movie *Her*, Samantha, the intelligent computer operating system, eloquently states, "The past is just a story that we tell ourselves." Isn't that powerful? Think about that for a second. We control how we interpret for a second. We control how we interpret past experiences. If we believe this is true, then what is stopping us from telling a more powerful, passionate story to ourselves? What's the best story that you'll tell yourself today to move forward?

EXERCISE #3

"Turning the obstacle upside down" is a favorite exercise by Marcus Aurelius (and more recently, Ryan Holiday. Thanks, Ryan), and it is the best way to frame obstacles and turn them to your advantage. It's simple: There's some obstacle...some bad situation that you're facing. Your crush doesn't have the same feelings for you as you do for her. Your bike gets hit by a car. You have no right hand. Now, imagine that this obstacle is a test from life. The "gods" are testing you. Now the question becomes this: "What's the test, and how do I beat it?" What qualities do you need to gain, practice, and cultivate in order to persevere and beat the test?

Let's address the three issues put forth above.

YOUR CRUSH DOESN'T HAVE THE SAME FEELINGS FOR YOU AS YOU DO FOR HER

Stoic response: That person is actually directing you toward a new path—one in which you will become a better boyfriend or girlfriend based on the things you learned in the previous relationship.

YOUR BIKE GETS HIT BY A CAR

Stoic response: Whether or not the fault was yours or that of the operator of the vehicle, maybe there are other ways to travel to your destination. In exploring the new route, maybe you'll appreciate the natural surroundings or increase the length of your route, causing you to get more exercise.

NO RIGHT HAND

Stoic response: In many ways, no right hand can make me better than those with two hands. I've learned to problem solve by coming up with ways to play baseball better than others. I'm more creative, and I've built resilience that will benefit me in clutch situations.

See what I mean?

This exercise helps in one key way: As you develop this practice into a habit, you are able to turn bad situations into good situations. They become opportunities. This feeds upon our work with mind-set and process.

EXERCISE #4

Exercise #4 is a mental technique by Sebastian Marshall called "The Player 1 Exercise." Here is how it goes:

1. Say you do poorly at your first recital. Instead of saying, "Oh screw piano; I hate this," take a step back and imagine if you were playing a video game and you were dropped in as Player 1.
2. How would it feel? Then act accordingly.
3. Brainstorm a list of ten things that are bothering you, and be honest: Is this thing within your control or outside it?
4. Then elaborate. If it's within your control, how can you make it better? Start seeing where you can control the variables, and then get to work.

CHAPTER 8

THE SCIENCE OF SELF-AWARENESS

"I have been and still am a seeker, but I have ceased to question stars and books; I have begun to listen to the teaching my blood whispers to me."

— HERMANN HESSE

Growing up as an Italian, Vince Lombardi faced an immense amount of racism as a young kid in 1920s New York City. He quickly learned to use struggle as fuel, leading him to Fordham University as an undersized offensive lineman. Lombardi knew he was not the most talented kid in the locker room, but he worked well with his team, and he left his heart out on the field. After years on the gridiron, Lombardi became a local football celebrity at Fordham, all while the school became a powerhouse that was well respected and well known for its impeccable offensive line known as "The Seven Blocks of Granite." Eventually, "The Seven Blocks of Granite" became known throughout New York City and the United States as one of the best offensive lines in history.

Lombardi graduated and moved on to become a high school coach and teacher. And while it wasn't the NFL, he loved every minute of the game. After twenty years of limited attention, moving onto Fordham, then West Point, and having no real prospects for a head-coaching job, he finally moved on professionally as an assistant in the NFL. During his first year with the New York Giants, Lombardi was eager to establish himself as an authority figure—as someone to listen to. But it didn't work as he intended.

He was unusually hard on the players, and he treated them like college students, which was a coaching style that did not gel well with the players. With Lombardi's awkward brand of hard-assery, the players didn't take him seriously, and for his first year at the NFL, they showed him no respect. For Lombardi, it was unbearable. Until, of course, he changed his tactics.

During training camp, Lombardi roamed the dorms, acknowledging both honestly and openly that he had much to learn. He consulted the players for advice on how to be better. Lombardi knew that if he could earn the respect of the player leadership, then he could begin to rebuild his image and strategy with the players. Lombardi sought out future Hall of Fame running back Frank Gifford. And Gifford, leader of the team at the time, began to notice, and with due time, appreciate the coach's efforts. Soon, he rallied his team around Lombardi, and their relationship became a collaborative effort and one in which Lombardi listened to his players and his players listened to him.

Lombardi persisted and adjusted, becoming a successful offensive coordinator with the Giants and leading the team to an NFL championship in 1956. In 1959, Vince Lombardi became the head coach of the Green Bay Packers. At forty-six years old, he was finally running his own team. At that point in history, the Green Bay Packers was a team that nobody wanted to coach. But despite his own eastern inclinations, something in Lombardi understood the gravity of the opportunity: It was a chance to redefine himself and take up the reins like he always wanted. At the beginning of 1961, he changed the direction of the team. After a critical loss in the season, he told his players in the locker room, including Bart Starr, who was quarterback at the time, "They beat us today, but this will never happen to us again."

His prediction came true. From there on out, Lombardi and Co. ended up winning numerous championships, including wins in the first two Super Bowls ever. He would go down as one of the greatest coaches in NFL history. And as confident as he was, even growing up as a small Italian kid in NYC, Lombardi developed a keen sense of self-awareness. He always asked himself, "How can I be better?" It was this constant desire to improve that gave him his first Super Bowl win in 1966 against the Kansas City Chiefs and, eventually, famously had his name engraved onto the official Super Bowl trophy.

WHAT IT MEANS TO BE SELF-AWARE

So what made Lombardi so great? How did self-awareness become such a powerful tool in his life? Vince Lombardi was, in short, great at introspection. Self-awareness is the capacity for introspection. It is a critical but fair self-diagnosis. Natalie Boyd discusses this brilliantly in her Psychology 104: Social Psychology course. Imagine this scenario: You're living in a beautiful Victorian house. You're looking out from that house, and you see this beautiful green lawn. You're near a mountain range that's majestic. Maple trees line the streets. Birds are chirping, and there is an occasional passerby. Now, you look inside your home: There's furniture, wood, carpet, candles, and the occasional family member. Somehow, staring out through the window, you forget what you own—what's yours—until it fades into the background. That's the difference between introspection and outward observation. Human beings have a tendency to not do enough introspection. In fact, it's an ingrained tendency of ours to do more outward observation rather than evaluating our own thoughts, feelings, and motives.

The beeper study illustrates this point perfectly. For a data set, the researchers gave a bunch of subjects a beeper. Every time the beeper went off, they would have to write down exactly what they were thinking at that moment. Surprisingly, for the entire data set, only roughly 8% of the observations ended up being introspective, whereas a whopping 92% were outward. Anybody who is able to do effective introspection is able to see exactly who they are, what they're about, and where they've fallen short. If you are trying to become a better baseball player, watch a tape of yourself. Try to provide an unbiased perspective on what you observe to be good and bad. Then how do you improve? What action do you need to take? If you're trying to improve your baseball game, you self-diagnose your strengths and your weaknesses and make a judgment call on what you need to do.

Whether it's laziness, an inability to look inward, or simply self-delusion acting as a self-defense mechanism, it's easy to have a false sense of awareness. For Lombardi to be keenly aware of the lack of respect he was getting in his first year—with an NFL franchise team no less—showed not only bravery but also an impeccable self-awareness (a situation in which most people would try to delude themselves out of their insecurity). The truth is, we delude ourselves all the time. It's much easier and much more comfortable to blame other people than it is to diagnose yourself. On the same side of the coin, it's also dangerous to be hypercritical of yourself—looking too much into your motives, your thoughts, and your feelings, especially if you don't know how to utilize them in the right way. Constantly being introspective and missing out on the things in front of you can become a recipe for depression and shame. The good news is that the downside of too much introspection can be negated by the growth mind-set. "I have negatives" or "I have shortcomings" doesn't become a painful problem for someone with a growth mind-set. Instead, it becomes a learning opportunity, and the thought loops in your head become much more manageable: "Okay, I have shortcomings. What do I do to fix them?"

EXERCISE #5

In the book by Dr. Jim Afremow, *The Champion's Mind*, he evaluates the differences between average athletes and great athletes. Afremow believes that the key to change—to improve from average to good and from good to great—is self-awareness. Being able to gauge both shortcomings and strengths is a principal ingredient in athletic development. "Today is what gets us to tomorrow," Afremow writes. To get to such a high level of self-awareness, athletes analyzed their daily performance to figure out where they went right and where they went wrong. In *The Champion's Mind*, one way in which athletes were able to improve their sustainable performance was by using a well-worn tactic: visualization.

How do we successfully visualize? Here's how to take action:

1. Visualize yourself in the target environment. *Example: You are making a sales presentation to a Fortune 500 CEO.*
2. While there are many techniques, one successful technique is utilizing mental imagery. According to Dr. Aymeric Guillot, scientists believe that we may experience real-world and imaginary actions in similar ways. *Example: You are dressed well, speaking clearly, engaging the audience, and by the end of the presentation, your customer has been so impressed that he has signed a contract right after the presentation.*
3. Whether it's writing a book, making a game-winning catch, or creating a beautiful piece of art, being able to visualize success helps you actualize it. You might not be able to create the exact

circumstances in real life, but visualizing helps you build a layer of unshakable confidence for any situation, whether it's a game, book, or project. The more vividly you visualize, the greater the benefit you reap.

EXERCISE #6

So, how do we build self-awareness? Building your self-awareness muscle is a natural extension of learning how to focus on what you can control (Chapter 7). Here is one exercise that helps me to practice self-awareness:

1. Goal: Pick one goal you are working on for tomorrow. This could be a workout, a meal, or a new morning routine you are trying to implement. Write it down.
2. Measure: How will you measure its success? If it is a workout, maybe there is a time element (thirty minutes), calories burned, or sufficiently working out certain muscle groups. It could be all of the above. Write it down.
3. Reflection: Once you complete the task, take ten minutes to reflect on it.
4. Question: If you met the requirements of your goal, did you challenge yourself accordingly? If you didn't meet the goal, what action do you need to take to reach it tomorrow? Do you need to build in supports (accountability partner, mentor, or online group) who can help you reach your goals?

The idea is to develop the habit of questioning your thoughts and opinions. This is not meant to beat up on yourself. Be critical, but be fair. Praise what is worth praising. The goal is improvement, not bashing.

CHAPTER 9

THE CLARITY OF PURPOSE

"He who has a why to live for can bear almost any how."

— FRIEDRICH NIETZSCHE

On November 12, 1976, college basketball player Terry Fox went for a drive. While distracted by nearby construction, the young student, just shy of nineteen, smashed into the back of a pickup truck. His life would be changed forever.

Fox grew up in a supportive, nurturing household. His mother instilled the values of drive and passion at an early age, and for Fox, the message stuck. But while his work ethic might've been undeniable, as an 8th grader at five feet tall, he simply wasn't good enough to play until his sophomore year of high school. During his senior year, Fox eventually became athlete of the year and developed into an accomplished basketball player. Because of his size, Terry's coaches believed his future in basketball looked bleak. "Why don't you take up cross country?" his coach remarked. Out of respect for his coach, he started running.

At Simon Fraser University, Fox walked onto the team as a freshman and was able to play junior varsity. But during that stint, on November 12, 1976, while taking a casual drive, Terry Fox smashed into the back of a pickup truck. His truck was totaled, yet Fox emerged from the smoking car with only a sore knee. He started to feel more and more pains in his right leg as the days went on. And while Terry wasn't one to complain, the pain reached boiling point: He couldn't move his right leg, and the swelling became unbearable. He was forced into the hospital. As an eighteen-year-old athlete, anything short of recovery felt like an impossible reality to grip. The prognosis was devastating. Terry Fox was diagnosed with cancer in his right leg, and the only course of action was to amputate. For Fox, this was devastating.

While Terry grew up in a nice neighborhood with a strong family and experienced success, cancer was never something he had to worry about. But lying in the hospital bed, his leg removed due to the cancer, it became all he could think about. From the young to the old, Fox developed relationships with fellow cancer patients, many of whom suffered immensely. Some died. These experiences served as a catalyst for Fox to do something about it.

Right before his leg was amputated, someone had given him an article of Dick Traum, who in 1976, famously ran the New York City Marathon with one leg. Fox's eyes had immediately lit up. After the amputation, Fox decided to run a marathon in the next twelve to fourteen months. With the support of his friends, especially Doug Alward (who made the trek with him), he focused on raising $1 million for cancer research by starting the Marathon of Hope. Initially, though, Fox was met with fierce criticism. No one would fund him. And at one point, the Canadian Cancer Society almost took his proposal as a joke.

Terry Fox started anyway. Learning how to run—with a prosthetic, no less—was difficult starting out. Along each run, the prosthetic would grind into his nub. Terry fell over and over again. He kept getting up. But with an attitude that surprised even his coach, his running got better. Fox realized that after twenty minutes, he reached a pain threshold and it became easier to persist. Eventually, Fox was able to hold his ground.

During the Marathon of Hope, Fox covered an impressive 3,339 miles of running in 143 days. That is over twenty-three miles per day through intense pain and adverse conditions. Feeling sorry for yourself? Fox blasted through his $1 million dollar goal and turned that into $10 million. As he traveled across Canada, he challenged his fellow countrymen to donate $1 for cancer research (there were 24 million Canadians at the time). The cancer returned, dashing his hopes of completing the journey. His motivation was inspiring: "I don't feel that this is unfair. That's the thing about cancer. I am not the only one. It happens all the time to people." He had found a calling to him that was higher than becoming a high school athlete. And as a direct result of the $650 million he'd go on to raise, the cure rates for osteosarcoma have increased to 80% in younger patients. Today, he is a celebrated hero in Canada.

A HIGHER PURPOSE

In 1972, Victor Frankl was taught a valuable lesson by his

flying instructor. "If you want to get from point A to point B," the instructor said, drawing a large dot on the board, "you cannot get there by flying straight. There's a crosswind, and if you went completely straight, you wouldn't end up at your destination." So to compensate, the instructor told Frankl to aim further north. The moral of the story is that life is not about getting from point A to point B. We likely would not reach our mark. Adjust for the crosswind, the obstacles, barriers, and adversity that are a part of the journey. Even if you overestimate (adjusting for the crosswind) and shoot higher, you're not only likely to hit point B but to get a little further. Frankl used this story to emphasize the importance of attacking life with a sense of purpose, building toward something bigger than yourself, and providing value to others and yourself.

Viktor Frankl is the author of the highly acclaimed classic, *Man's Search for Meaning*, which is a story about his experience at the Auschwitz concentration camp. Based on his gut-wrenching experience, Frankl posed the question: How do we find meaning in the direst of circumstances? Much of the theory he espouses in the book he formed through his own study of logotherapy and existential analysis. During his years at Auschwitz, Frankl, a prisoner and therapist who treated his inmates, realized that the people who survived weren't the strongest or even the most optimistic. Instead, they were the people with a definitive "why" in their life. They did not ignore their situation, but they exercised resilience because of a sense of responsibility to serve something greater. For Frankl himself, it was this sense of higher meaning that propelled him throughout the book. Frankl felt a responsibility to write a book to share with the world his theory on logotherapy. Years later, his story provided a platform for his research and allowed the book to be read by over five million people worldwide.

THE LIFESTYLES WE LEAD

Dr. Martin Seligman, widely known as the father of positive psychology, breaks life down into three lifestyles: the pleasant life, the good life, and the meaningful life. The pleasant life is achieved through realizing basic pleasures: environment, comfortable shelter, and relationships. Sometimes, it can lead to superficiality and greed. The pleasant life is based on comfort and superficial pleasure. Idealizing movie stars and focusing on money, success, and fame can be indicators of someone living the pleasant life. For 50% of Americans, it's completely heritable. A pleasant life is a mile wide and an inch deep in happiness and engagement.

Then, there's the good life—the life that provides engagement. Seligman challenges us to imagine this: You've got an options trader friend who is also a successful bridge champion. But he's terrible with relationships. So the question is, is he living a good life? Some people would say, no, of course not; a person needs love to become truly fulfilled. However, this man isn't looking for love. Instead, he's looking for a life of engagement, and his goal is fulfilled through being an options trader and a bridge champion. This is the essence of the good life. It's a life achieved through the discovery of our core strengths and unique virtues and applying them to enhance our lives.

Then, there's the meaningful life, which is when you infuse

a high sense of purpose with an understanding of our unique strengths and virtues. It's when you're working toward something that's bigger than yourself, and you're working toward something that's going to make a difference not just for you but in other people's lives. It's the difference between selling widgets and using your selling skills to acquire funding to build schools in sub-Saharan Africa. It could mean spending an hour a week on the side working at a local soup kitchen. This is ultimate fulfillment.

Of course, Seligman also surprisingly offers another lifestyle—the full life—which is a combination and intersection of the previous three. It's a life that maintains a successful stasis between the surface-level wants, the engagement, and then the search for meaning. The opposite is aptly titled the empty life, which is when parts of the equation are missing. This is what you don't want. Instead, you want a full life. You want a life in which your needs are met, you're engaging with the world, and you're attacking each day with a sense of mission and purpose to contribute to your community and the world.

To access a higher purpose and get closer to an ideal, full life, here are two exercises.

EXERCISE #7

1. Take out a piece of paper and a pen or pencil.
2. Ask yourself, "What inspires me to show up in life?"
3. Answer in as much detail as you can and then elaborate. Push yourself to write for thirty minutes. You will approach a wall, but you need to persist to unlock your deeper details of purpose.
4. Leave it for the day, and put it somewhere you will see it the following morning.
5. The next morning, reflect on what you've written down. If your answers don't match what you are currently doing, then start to architect small ways to integrate the first one or two into your life.

Are you happy at work? Are you unhappy at work? If you're unhappy, why do you wake up and do it? What really fills you up? It's invaluable for you to be self-critical and to crystallize what you want.

EXERCISE #8

Imagine you are going to die in six months. Imagine your network of friends and family was told that you'd be gone.

1. The person you love is told that in six months, you'll be lowered, six feet under. Really feel it.
2. Now ask yourself: What do you want to do before you die? With six months to live, our purpose isn't obfuscated by the momentum of our lives. Instead, it's clarified. Ask yourself, what would you really do?
3. Light a fire. Start to integrate that first thought into your daily life.

This doesn't mean quitting your job. This doesn't mean going Dave Chappelle on us and moving to Africa for months. The exercise is designed to get you thinking deeply about doing something worth doing. If we aren't, then we can take the first small action to get there.

CHAPTER 10

STANDING ON THE SHOULDERS OF GIANTS

"Great heroes need great sorrows and burdens, or half their greatness goes unnoticed. It is all part of the fairy tale."

— PETER S. BEAGLE, THE LAST UNICORN

Bill Belichick grew from humble beginnings. His Croatian grandparents immigrated to the US, had five kids, worked blue-collar jobs, and were poor for the majority of their lives. However, they lived the American dream. Steve Belichick, Bill's father, served in the US Army and became an assistant football coach for the U.S. Naval Academy. Paradoxically, Steve never aspired or wanted to be a head football coach; he valued time with his family too highly to travel. Bill, as a young kid, became an extension of his father: When Steve studied film, Bill watched film. When Steve had practice, Bill would do everything he could to watch practice. He loved every aspect of the game. Being the inquisitive kid he was, he constantly asked his father questions about football. And growing up, Bill learned all he could from breaking down game film to meeting the players themselves. As Malcolm Gladwell writes in *Outliers*, it was no wonder that Bill accumulated his 10,000 hours. His exposure to all facets of the game gave Belichick a perspective that most players and coaches don't have an opportunity to experience.

From high school to Wesleyan University (my alma mater!), Bill played football and lacrosse, yet he quickly realized in college that his heart just wasn't in playing. Instead, it was in coaching. And as he learned more and more about the complexities of the game, it was the closeness with his father, as well as their love of football, that made the mentor relationship especially fruitful throughout his later years. Belichick, as we know him today, is the head coach of the New England Patriots and is now a veteran coach. With all of Belichick's success, he believes he owes much to the opportunities provided to him.

He stands on the shoulders of giants for many reasons: the fortitude of his grandparents emigrating to the US; the coaches, owners, and players who developed the game of football into the sport it is today; and the people in history who have allowed us to be free and safe and who have paved the way for the pursuit of happiness. It was and is the culmination of the supporting cast around him that helped him become the man he is today.

STANDING ON THE SHOULDERS OF GIANTS

Growing up, Benny DiNardo, my grandfather, led anything but a charmed life. He was one of twelve children, and his parents emigrated from Italy to Ellis Island in the late 1800s. With a twenty-five-year difference between the oldest and youngest siblings, he developed into a man quickly. Living below their means, he was forced to work in the coal mines but still managed to stay active and play baseball and football. Then, World War II hit, and Benny DiNardo enlisted in the army. Times were a-changin'. At twenty-six, as Benny approached the beaches of Normandy, he saw the quiet panic that washed over his friends in the throes of death. Benny and his comrades spoke of death on that boat ride. Whenever I see the first scene in *Saving Private Ryan*, I picture what it might have been like to approach those beaches and react as the door swung open to bullets whizzing by his head. But as fate would have it, he survived. Later, he would go on to become a colonel and then a brigadier general and tour the world, traveling all the way from Greece, Germany, and Monterey, California, and eventually settling down in North Attleboro, Massachusetts. He was even lucky enough to get a picture of him—just a simple kid from Ellsworth, Pennsylvania—shaking the hand of the King of Greece.

Growing up, my grandfather never bragged, even though he had plenty to brag about, such as the purple heart he received after saving a few men from a tank right before it exploded and shrapnel pierced his arms or the silver star and two bronze medals he received after years of service. Until he passed away, I never found out because I never asked, and he never mentioned them. He was humble, and I always had the sense that he didn't yearn for credit, accolades, or thank-yous. All he did was lead a life that was meaningful to him. And I respected the hell out of that.

What inspires me about my grandfather is that he not only helped me live the life I'm living today but also that his adversity is so much bigger than anything I've ever faced. And that moves me. Not only did he grow up in rising early America, work the coal mines, and get thrust into the heart of World War II, but he also successfully raised a family that would eventually come to raise me. He was the catalyst that took the DiNardos from lower-class immigrants to the comforts of the middle class. And, in retrospect, I came to see it as my responsibility to carry on his legacy, build a life of meaning that builds pride within our family, and serve as a model for my future children.

It's beautiful to think that there were trillions of tiny events that led to this very moment. And it's important to understand that life is much bigger than you. Whether you know it or not, there are people inside and outside your family who've set the stage for you to pursue the things you're passionate about. And there will be more people in your future who'll change the course of your life just like those in the past have done. The main point of all this is that standing on the stories and shoulders of giants helps us deal with adversity because it helps us tell ourselves that if they can do it, so can we. In a very real sense, most of our heroes are our heroes because we see our potential embedded inside them.

EXERCISE #9

Have you ever done research on someone in your family history? How much do you know about your dad? What about that great-uncle you never met but heard some interesting war stories about?

1. Pick a family member you are interested in finding out more about.
2. Become an investigator. Do some research. Contact relatives, scour the Internet (Ancestry.com could be a great catalyst), interview the actual person, and compile the information.
3. Many times, you'll be surprised to find out that many people in your family actually went through a lot.

So appreciate all the things that got you here, including your uncles, aunts, and cousins. Use their stories and struggles as mental fuel to get you through tough times.

EXERCISE #10

1. Dig into the story of one person you admire from afar. It can be a celebrity, a politician, or a writer.

2. After a few hours of research, you'll notice that most of our heroes aren't the superhumans we make them out to be in our heads or those in the sensationalized media. They make mistakes. They try their best. They were awkward teenagers who didn't know what they wanted to do with the rest of their lives. And it can be not only humbling but also incredibly liberating to realize that you can be one of them. Seeing our heroes as simply one of us doesn't just humanize them; it instills a sense that, given the right tools, we can grow. It helps us appreciate the greats who came before and it reinforces a growth mindset. From reading biographies and watching documentaries to listening to stories and recording interviews, presidents and CEOs have used the stories of others to motivate them. Whether it's about politics, sports, European history, scientists, or your family, find the stories that move you, and use them as fuel. If they can do it, so can you.

CHAPTER 11

WHAT IT TAKES TO BE COOL

"Give me six hours to chop down a tree and I will spend the first four sharpening the axe."

— ABRAHAM LINCOLN

At the age of six, Arthur Ashe's mother died from complications during pregnancy. His father, though illiterate and largely uneducated, did his best to raise him, pushing him toward the education that he himself had never gotten. The civil rights movement was in full swing, and young, black Arthur Ashe, now a student on a sports scholarship to UCLA, was dominating an almost entirely white pastime: tennis. Though the animosity in the south reached intolerable levels, Arthur Ashe was excelling through his talent, dedication, and hallmark poise for coolness under pressure. Within a few years, Ashe became internationally renowned. He was the first prominent black tennis player, the first black player selected to the US Davis Cup team, and the only black man to have won the singles titles at Wimbledon, the US Open, and the Australian Open grand slams combined. He would later be declared one of the top twenty players to ever play the sport.

Ashe suffered a heart attack at age 36. It was revealed that his mother and father experienced serious heart problems, and Ashe's emerging heart issues were hereditary. It forced him from the game he loved, and he retired in 1979. He found out that he had toxoplasmosis, a parasitic infection common to those with compromised immune systems, often from HIV. Ashe was devastated. The blood transfusions he had received after his second heart surgery, intended to be life and career saving, were his death warrant. It must have felt as if the universe was conspiring against him.

Initially, Ashe kept the HIV diagnosis a secret. He was concerned about how others would view him and about the effects on his family. But Ashe eventually came out to his family and the public as HIV positive. He began ardently advocating for AIDS research and prevention. His advocacy focused heavily on children, especially inner-city youth. He promoted safe sex, education, and the importance of thinking intelligently about these issues.

Ashe was later invited to speak at the Connecticut Forum on February 6, 1993. Due to life-threatening pneumonia, he was unable to attend, but he submitted—unexpectedly—a video sharing some of his thoughts. In the video, Ashe in a violet sweater, gaunt and thin, spoke in measured tones about many things, including the realities of urban youth and peer pressure. He had used the platform as a means to educate the public on the social causes he was passionate about. Though his body had withered away, his calm, controlled personality was evident. And then, around the intermission at the Connecticut Forum, Arthur Ashe passed away.

COOLNESS AND WHAT IT ALL MEANS

Arthur Ashe carried himself the way he played tennis—with serenity and grace. Whether he was facing tennis giants, such as Jimmy Connors and Bjorn Borg, in the 1970s or talking to inner-city youth, his ability to be cool and even-keeled under pressure was his greatest and most crucial asset.

Like Ashe, NFL quarterback Joe Montana exuded the same shade of cool that led Ashe to so many wins. At Super Bowl XXIII, down 16–13 with only three minutes left on the clock and ninety-two yards from the goal line, the San Francisco 49ers offense huddled up. One of his tackles lined up to start the play. Suddenly, Montana noticed celebrity John Candy in the stands. Right as they were about to start the drive, Montana casually remarked to his blocker, Harris Barton, "Hey... is that John Candy in the stands?" Everyone within earshot glanced over; Harris Barton was bewildered. *How could Montana be so nonchalant in the final moments of the most important game of their lives?* After eleven plays and roughly three minutes, Montana threw a swift pass to John Taylor to complete a 92 yard drive. Touchdown, 49ers. They won the Super Bowl.

When you're a quarterback faced with a series of intense, game-breaking decisions, it's crucial to find a cool head. Tom Brady, starting quarterback for the New England Patriots, explained this in an interview with WEEI.com: "I've been around for a little bit, so I've been in these situations. Good execution usually solves a lot of the issues. When you're not executing well, you don't score many points. I think you're just trying to focus really on the situation, not what has happened over the course of the game. You get in a situation where you need a touchdown at the end, that's the situation you're in. You talk about those situations, you go through in your head the types of plays you're going to run, the types of reads I'm going to make, the types of defense you're going to see. Everyone does that, from the quarterback to the offensive line, and we have meetings about those types of things, so when those situations come up, no one is really surprised. You're just focused on what you need to do and you go out there and try to execute it."

This doesn't mean cool like "The Fonz"; it means poised, prepared, and ready. The secret of being cool isn't just trying to *be cool*. Preparation creates coolness. Ever study so much for a test that when you took it, it felt uncharacteristically easy? When people are prepared, it feels easy—as it should. When we are unprepared, anxiety can eat us for dinner. From a cognitive perspective, researchers understand that anxiety increases fear and apprehension, which can cloud our judgment. The goal should be to keep the mind free from anxiety. We can exert control through the quality of our preparation for events that may trigger this anxiety. Understanding the importance of preparation is supported by two of our other components: growth mind-set and respect for the process. Athletes need to prepare mentally, physically, and strategically in order to be truly prepared. For Joe Montana, preparation meant research on the opposing defense and what their tendencies were against certain offensive formations at different points in a game. He wanted to understand every player's strengths and weaknesses.

The greatest athletes are the ones who are focused on preparing for adversity, not avoiding it. Seneca explains in *Letters from a Stoic* the importance of putting yourself into bad situations as an opportunity to be better. The simple fact is that the more you expose yourself to pressure, even in the general sense, the better prepared you are to be cool under it.

In sports lexicon, one concept that is under constant debate is whether or not a player can "be clutch." When Joe Montana threw the game-winning touchdown in Super Bowl 23, that was clutch. Jeff Wise broke down specifically the science of clutch. In an article titled "The Science of Sports: Is there Such a Thing as a Clutch Performer?", Wise describes athletic performance under two types of skills: gross motor skills and fine motor skills. Gross motor skills are bigger movements by larger muscles (e.g., running and punching), and fine motor skills are smaller movements by smaller muscles (e.g., shooting a basketball and hitting a baseball). But when you shoot a basketball, that's a fine-tuned motor skill. What makes the distinction is the role pressure plays here.

Say you're running away from a bear. The fact that pressure is applied, and that you're literally running for your life, makes you run faster than you normally would. Why are almost all world records broken at the Olympics? Pressure contributes to increased performance with gross motor skills—up to a point. In Wise's research, the graph is an inverse U, where stress can increase performance to a certain extent and then, at an inflection point, it begins to erode. That's when athletes begin to "choke." Under high-stress situations, performance is extreme: great performance and poor performance. "The difference," as Wise puts it, "seems to be the amount of training the person has. Like gross motor skills, very well learned skills seem to thrive under intense pressure." The more work you put into skill development, the better you'll be under pressure when the stakes are high. Exposure to the situation creates a coolness with the situation itself.

So how do we achieve "being cool"? The science is clear: Poise comes from confidence, which comes from targeted preparation. Therefore, if you want to be cool under pressure, you need to respect the process through mental and physical practice and training (however that may look for your activity) in order to sharpen your performance. Targeted preparation alone isn't enough, though. Instead, you'll need to sync targeted performance with the internal shift that causes confidence. Mostly, this process is a natural shift since once you show ability in something, you invest your confidence in it. Confidence is a by-product of time and skill development. So just take the first step.

EXERCISE #11

CREATING A PREPARATION PLAN

Practice creating a preparation plan. The act of writing down and sequencing the tactics for what needs to be accomplished will create this inner confidence. For example, want to perform in that fifty-mile cycling challenge? It won't happen overnight. Here are some examples of preparation:

1. Understanding the timeline: When is the race? Backward-design

your goals, and break them into weekly and monthly targets. If the race is six months away, maybe the first week you start with four rides of five miles a piece. If you increase this by a mile every week until the race date, you'll be at thirty-one miles per day. Backward design is essential for wrapping your mind around aspirations.

2. Equipment: Does your bike meet the minimum requirements to perform? Consistently check the tires, frame, brakes, and so on.
3. Develop the habit: Just ride. Work to achieve consistency. From there, you can start to add daily scheduling and meal changes to improve your performance.
4. Mirror the best: Read, watch videos, and listen to podcasts on what competitive cyclists do, or it could just be regular Joes who like to raise money for charity. Whatever works.

This is just an example of how to develop a preparation plan. It can be as holistic or linear as you'd like. The goal, if you are serious about achieving what you set out to do, is to think these details through to improve your confidence.

EXERCISE #12

BREATHING

Another technique from researchers and practitioners is to focus on breathing. Focusing on breathing slows you down; it allows you to slow your mind, slow the game down, and think through situations clearly. Tim Ferriss, multiple New York Times bestselling author, has personally touched on meditation as being the key to a clear, concentrated mind. Whether it's ten to fifteen minutes a day of meditation or silently focusing on your breathing in a public situation, anyone can access the benefits of mindfulness.

EXERCISE #13

For the last exercise to tie it up, raising the stakes is a great strategy to execute under pressure. Say you want to run a marathon but you're not a runner. Well, you've got a year ahead of you, so it's time to set up some stakes. In a month, it makes sense to set up a 5k, where you're now committed to going with friends. Now, if you tread back on your word and don't do the 5k, you risk social embarrassment. At the same time, that pressure helps you get focused, tie up your shoelaces, and start running. Then, it's all a matter of each month, in each segment you decide, to up the stakes until, finally, you're ready to run a marathon. And, after you've accomplished your goal—whatever that is—reflect on the experience and diagnose where you went right and where you went wrong, and go from there.

CHAPTER 12

THE IMPORTANCE OF FEELING LUCKY

"Do not spoil what you have by desiring what you have not; remember that what you now have was once among the things you only hoped for."

— EPICURUS

Long before Lou "Iron Horse" Gehrig became one of the most prominent figures in American baseball history, he was just a poor boy from Yorkville, Manhattan. He was the only surviving son of four born to German immigrants. Neither of his parents was college-educated, which spurred his mother to push Lou toward getting a degree. At Columbia University, Gehrig, always with a winning attitude, showed an incredible aptitude and attitude for baseball. His ability to understand the game, with its intricacies and quirks, outpaced even his peers'.

Much of Lou's life was fueled by immense gratitude for the opportunities he had. He felt a responsibility to take advantage of every day. He was seemingly indestructible, even being called by columnist Jim Murray a "Gibraltar in cleats," and he played through pain and injury, suffering seventeen different fractures during the streak. Even then, Gehrig was able to play a whopping total of 2,130 games. Gehrig had an inviolate gratitude that permeated every aspect of his life. He recognized that he had been given opportunities through fortitude and fortune that others only dreamed of. And for the Iron Horse, rising from the hovels of poverty in early America, he felt especially lucky to not only just play baseball but also to play it for a living. Injuries were a minor hurdle compared to what others dealt with every day in America.

In 1939, Lou Gehrig was diagnosed with ALS, a neurodegenerative disease that affects the nerve cells in the brain and spinal cord. There was no cure then; there is no cure now. The average survival from onset to death is three to four years, with merely 4% of patients surviving longer than ten years. ALS ended Lou Gehrig's career and, two years later, his life. But it did not change who he was. In 1939, Lou Gehrig said goodbye to baseball with a speech that would go down in American history. At his farewell address, Lou Gehrig spoke with a keen, unwavering gratitude:

"Fans, for the past two weeks you have been reading about the bad break I got. Yet today I consider myself the luckiest man on the face of this earth. I have been in ballparks for seventeen years and have never received anything but kindness and encouragement from you fans...When you have a father and a mother who work all their lives so you can have an education and build your body, it's a blessing.

When you have a wife who has been a tower of strength and shown
more courage than you dreamed existed, that's the finest I know. So
I close in saying that I might have been given a bad break, but I've
got an awful lot to live for."

THE IMPORTANCE OF GRATITUDE

Research tells us that gratitude is an emotion that expresses
appreciation for what one has rather than what one wants.
But what empirical evidence shows us is that it can be cultivated. It isn't something you're born with, but rather a practice
and a habit born from intention. When we do become more
grateful, the evidence is clear: We become happier and have
increased levels of energy, optimism, and empathy. Like Lou
Gehrig, even through the greatest adversity, it is our choice
to approach obstacles with gratitude. Is it easy? No. Counting
our blessings while learning from our failures is hard to do.
But it's certainly possible, achievable, and worthwhile.

EXERCISE #14

This exercise forces us to unlock emotions that we may not access or may have avoided. It is an opportunity to open our hearts and truly thank someone who has impacted our lives. Try it.

1. Close your eyes and think about someone in your life who is alive who has impacted you in a very close way.
2. Think hard about this person, and ask yourself why they've impacted you. Express that gratitude mentally.
3. Write a 300-word letter to them explaining what this person means to you.
4. Then, drive to their place and give them the note. If your person is not within driving distance, give them an impromptu telephone call and read the note.

EXERCISE #15

This exercise is from Leo Babauta at Zen Habits. It is extremely simple and effective to integrate into your life. It can be practiced in one of two methods.

1. The first is to be thankful every morning. Get into the habit of waking up every morning and spending two to three minutes thinking about what you are grateful for. You can think it or write it, but I suggest writing it down in the first seven to ten days of habit development. It's possible it might be difficult the first time, and you might not be able to come up with much initially. But each and every time, it will get easier; you will get better at it and begin your day positively, and this will reverberate throughout your entire day.
2. Start saying thank you. Your grandparents send you a gift, say thank you. Someone opens the door for you, say thank you. Someone emails you back, say thank you.
3. For the first week, log both the person's response and how you feel.

Over the past two decades, published studies of gratitude have grown significantly in number and credibility. From this research, we now know that saying "thank you" increases levels of happiness, improves relationships, and can lower blood pressure and strengthen your heart.

CHAPTER 13

LIFE, ADVERSITY, AND THE ROAD AHEAD

"Sweet are the uses of adversity which, like the toad, ugly and venomous, wears yet a precious jewel in his head."

— WILLIAM SHAKESPEARE

Life is a tricky thing. Many people have their own views about what it means and what it is. But I never thought life was necessarily about education. For me, I believe that life is more about doing our best to acquire wisdom. And the best way to do that is through life itself—through lived experience. When we face the hard things, it's our responsibility to face the hard things with the right response, to respond in the way we need to, to grow as a person, and to affect the world in a positive way. This response isn't something we can or should run away from. This response, and how we react to things, is essential and crucial for how our lives turn out. I believe life is defined by our ability to identify, respond to, and grow from adversity. Moments of adversity show themselves every day: large and small, important and trivial. Every moment of your life has the unique privilege of being part of who you are today: your memories, experiences, thoughts, and ideas.

In this book, my goal was to use sports stories as a vessel to educate and motivate you to look at adversity as a gift rather than something to avoid. Sports provides us with an amazing opportunity to learn about our character and how we have a choice to use these opportunities to grow or regress. My hypothesis was that adversity plays a crucial role in the success of most historically significant figures in various fields. The research I've done, and will continue to do, gives me confidence that this hypothesis is correct. Sports is a microcosm for life, and the skills we learn through playing, watching, and admiring these games do translate into our daily lives. I hope these stories, and the science and psychology behind them, inspire you to attack life's greatest challenges. I hope that this book gives you another perspective for taking action on goals you have yet to achieve. Thanks for the opportunity to show you what I believe. Now take on your next moment of adversity.

WHAT IF LIFE WERE PERFECT?

*What if you lived in a perfect world of perfect people
and perfect possessions, with everyone and everything
doing the perfect thing at the perfect time?*

*What if you had everything you wanted, and only what you
wanted, exactly as you wanted, precisely when you wanted it?*

*What if, after luxuriating in this perfect world for the
perfect length of time, you started feeling uneasy about the
predictability of perfection? What if, after an additional
perfect length of time, you began thinking, 'There seems
to be a lack of risk, adventure, and fun in perfection.
"Having it my way" all the time is getting dull.'*

*What if, after yet another perfect length of time,
you decided, 'Perfection is a perfect bore.'*

*What if, at that point in your perfect world, you
created a button marked, 'Surprise.'*

*What if you walked over, considered all that might be
contained in the concept of 'surprise,' decided, 'Anything's
better than boredom,' took a deep breath, pushed the button…*

*…and found yourself where you are right now—
feeling what you're feeling now, thinking what
you're thinking now, with everything in your life
precisely the way it is now—reading this book.*

{ PETER MCWILLIAMS }

THE THIRTY-DAY ADVERSITY CHALLENGE

"The philosophers have only interpreted the world, in various ways. The point, however, is to change it."

— KARL MARX

The only way to become better at using adversity to your advantage is through application. Experiential learning provides a powerful way to bring concepts into action. So let's dive into a program I've designed to help you build your adversity muscle.

Adversity is one of the greatest trainers you'll ever meet. It's time you take that message to heart and act on it. Here's a summary of all the exercises, in a concise, actionable thirty-day format so you can get started today. Do the exercises, reap the results. After you reach Day 30, restart from Day 22 (the plan gets personalized), and keep working on it until you're happy with a habit you've built. Then, move on to the next habit. It's that simple.

BUILDING BLOCKS

- Chapter 5: Growth Mind-set
- Chapter 6: Respect the Process
- Chapter 7: Focus on What You Can Control
- Chapter 9: Clarity of Purpose
- Chapter 10: Standing on the Shoulders of Giants
- Chapter 11: Be Cool
- Chapter 12: Gratitude

CHALLENGE BREAKDOWN

CHAPTER	BUILDING BLOCK	LENGTH
5	Growth Mind-Set	7 days
6	Process vs. Outcome	4 days
7	Focus/Control	3 days
8	Self-Awareness	4 days
9	Clarity of Purpose	3 days
10	Shoulders of Giants	2 days
11	Be Cool	2 days
12	Gratitude	4 days
	Postmortem	1 day

DAY 1

	RECORD	REFLECT	TOTAL
TIME INVESTMENT	1 minute	5 minutes	6 minutes

OBJECTIVE   LEARN TO HEAR YOUR "FIXED MIND-SET" VOICE

BUILDING BLOCKS   Mind-Set, Self-Awareness, Process, Focus/Control

INSTRUCTIONS   Read over Exercise #1. The goal today is to build small wins. Record yourself for one minute today. Talk to yourself about the good, the bad, and the ugly at work, in your relationship, and so on. Work to catch "fixed mind-set" talk.

DAY 2

BREATHING   TOTAL

	BREATHING	TOTAL
TIME INVESTMENT	10 minutes	10 minutes

OBJECTIVE   GRATITUDE

BUILDING BLOCKS   Gratitude, Shoulders of Giants, Mind-Set

INSTRUCTIONS   Complete Exercise #15: Thank You

DAY 3

RECORD   REFLECT   TOTAL

	RECORD	REFLECT	TOTAL
TIME INVESTMENT	1 minute	5 minutes	6 minutes

OBJECTIVE   LEARN TO HEAR YOUR "FIXED MIND-SET" VOICE

BUILDING BLOCKS   Mind-Set, Self-Awareness, Process, Focus/Control

INSTRUCTIONS   Repeat the exercise from Day 1. This time, there is a prompt involved. Think about a current project you are working on (work, house, athletics, art, etc.). Talk it through, and reflect on fixed mind-set talk.

DAY 4

	RECORD	REFLECT	TOTAL

TIME INVESTMENT	12 minutes	10 minutes	22 minutes
OBJECTIVE	LEARN TO HEAR YOUR "FIXED MIND-SET" VOICE		
BUILDING BLOCKS	Mind-Set, Self-Awareness, Process, Focus/Control		
INSTRUCTIONS	Complete the full version of Exercise #1. Try to record one minute/hour for twelve hours.		

DAY 5

	RECORD +LISTEN	REFLECT	TOTAL

TIME INVESTMENT	15 minutes	10 minutes	25 minutes
OBJECTIVE	CHOICE/TALKING BACK WITH A "GROWTH MIND-SET" VOICE		
BUILDING BLOCKS	Mind-Set, Self-Awareness, Process, Focus/Control		
INSTRUCTIONS	Go back to your recordings from days 1, 3 and 4. Recognize that you have a choice: to respond with growth mind-set "talk" or fixed mind-set talk. Practice by owning this choice, and write down your growth mind-set "talk" in opposition to your original fixed mind-set "talk."		

DAY 6

	RECORD +REFLECT	ACTION	TOTAL

TIME INVESTMENT	10 minutes	Depends on task	30–60 minutes
OBJECTIVE	TAKE GROWTH MIND-SET ACTION		
BUILDING BLOCKS	Mind-Set, Self-Awareness, Process, Focus/Control		
INSTRUCTIONS	Let's put it all together. Write down each circumstance when you have a "fixed mind-set" voice. Stop, acknowledge the choice, and talk back to it with a "growth mind-set" voice. Now, take action on the new, productive mind-set. For example, pissed off about having to do the dishes? Catch yourself; what could you say instead (I'm not giving you the answer!)? Now, take that positive action.		

DAY 7

RECORD   REFLECT   TOTAL

TIME INVESTMENT	10 minutes	10 minutes	20 minutes
OBJECTIVE	SETBACKS		
BUILDING BLOCKS	Mind-Set, Self-Awareness, Process, Focus/Control		
INSTRUCTIONS	What new challenges do you have coming up? Write one or two down. Think about the fixed mind-set "talk" and then apply the growth mind-set "talk." What is the difference in action?		

DAY 8

RECORD   REFLECT   TOTAL

TIME INVESTMENT	15 minutes	10 minutes	25 minutes
OBJECTIVE	NEW CHALLENGES		
BUILDING BLOCKS	Mind-Set, Self-Awareness, Process, Focus/Control		
INSTRUCTIONS	Read over Exercise #1. The goal today is to build small wins. Record yourself for one minute today. Talk to yourself about the good, the bad, and the ugly at work, in your relationship, and so on. Work to catch "fixed mind-set" talk.		

DAY 9

WATCH   TOTAL

TIME INVESTMENT	25 minutes	25 minutes
OBJECTIVE	UNDERSTAND THE IMPORTANCE OF PROCESS	
BUILDING BLOCKS	Mind-Set, Self-Awareness, Process, Focus/Control	
INSTRUCTIONS	Watch this YouTube video of Tim Ferriss explaining deconstruction. This, to me, is the essence of process. Go to thegameofadversity.com/tim to see the video.	

104 · THE GAME OF ADVERSITY

DAY 10

	TALK	BREAKDOWN	TOTAL
TIME INVESTMENT	10 minutes	20–30 minutes	30–40 minutes
OBJECTIVE	PRACTICE DECONSTRUCTION		
BUILDING BLOCKS	Process, Focus/Control, Be Cool		
INSTRUCTIONS	Read Exercise #2. Today, focus on identifying the goal you want to achieve, and break it down into its "parts." For example, a sales presentation includes (roughly) research, planning, development of a PowerPoint (or equivalent) presentation, practice, and presentation.		

DAY 11

	BREAKDOWN	TOTAL
TIME INVESTMENT	30–60 minutes	30–60 minutes
OBJECTIVE	PRACTICE DECONSTRUCTION	
BUILDING BLOCKS	Process, Focus/Control, Be Cool	
INSTRUCTIONS	Complete Exercise #2.	

DAY 12

	BREAKDOWN	TOTAL
TIME INVESTMENT	30–60 minutes	30–60 minutes
OBJECTIVE	PRACTICE DECONSTRUCTION	
BUILDING BLOCKS	Process, Focus/Control, Be Cool	
INSTRUCTIONS	Complete Exercise #2.	

DAY 13

	BREAKDOWN	TOTAL
TIME INVESTMENT	30 minutes	30 minutes
OBJECTIVE	PRACTICE FOCUSING ON WHAT WE CAN CONTROL	
BUILDING BLOCKS	Process, Focus/Control, Mind-Set, Be Cool	
INSTRUCTIONS	Complete Exercise #3: Turning the Obstacle Upside Down	

DAY 14

	BREAKDOWN	TOTAL
TIME INVESTMENT	30 minutes	30 minutes
OBJECTIVE	PRACTICE FOCUSING ON WHAT WE CAN CONTROL	
BUILDING BLOCKS	Process, Focus/Control, Mind-Set, Be Cool	
INSTRUCTIONS	Complete Exercise #3: Turning the Obstacle Upside Down	

DAY 15

	BREAKDOWN	TOTAL
TIME INVESTMENT	20 minutes	20 minutes
OBJECTIVE	PRACTICE FOCUSING ON WHAT WE CAN CONTROL	
BUILDING BLOCKS	Process, Focus/Control, Mind-Set, Be Cool	
INSTRUCTIONS	Complete Exercise #4: Player 1	

DAY 16

TIME INVESTMENT	5/10/10/10 minutes	35 min.
OBJECTIVE	UNDERSTANDING SELF-AWARENESS	
BUILDING BLOCKS	Mind-Set, Self-Awareness, Focus/Control	
INSTRUCTIONS	Complete Exercise #6: Self-Awareness	

DAY 17

TIME INVESTMENT	5/10/10/10 minutes	35 min.
OBJECTIVE	UNDERSTANDING SELF-AWARENESS	
BUILDING BLOCKS	Mind-Set, Self-Awareness, Focus/Control	
INSTRUCTIONS	Complete Exercise #6: Self-Awareness	

DAY 18 BREAKDOWN TOTAL

TIME INVESTMENT	20 minutes	20 minutes
OBJECTIVE	MID-GOAL REFLECTION	
BUILDING BLOCKS	Mind-Set, Self-Awareness	
INSTRUCTIONS	You are halfway to the thirty-day goal. Pat yourself on the back. It's not easy to get here. In 100–250 words, what have you learned? What do you still need to work on? Dig deep; you're doing great.	

DAY 19

	BREAKDOWN	TOTAL
TIME INVESTMENT	15–20 minutes	15–20 minutes
OBJECTIVE	PRACTICING SELF-AWARENESS	
BUILDING BLOCKS	Mind-Set, Self-Awareness, Focus/Control, Be Cool, Purpose	
INSTRUCTIONS	Complete Exercise #5: Visualization	

DAY 20

	VIDEO	WRITE	TOTAL
TIME INVESTMENT	28 minutes	20 minutes	48 minutes
OBJECTIVE	UNDERSTANDING THE IMPORTANCE OF PURPOSE		
BUILDING BLOCKS	Purpose, Focus/Control, Mind-Set, Standing on the Shoulders of Giants		
INSTRUCTIONS	Watch this video interview with Viktor Frankl, and write down a 250-word summary of your takeaways: thegameofadversity.com/viktor		

DAY 21

	WRITE	REFLECT	ACTION	TOTAL
TIME INVESTMENT	30 minutes	15 minutes	10 minutes	55 minutes
OBJECTIVE	PRACTICING PURPOSE			
BUILDING BLOCKS	Purpose, Focus/Control, Mind-Set, Standing on the Shoulders of Giants			
INSTRUCTIONS	Complete Exercise #7: Showing Up			

DAY 22

	WRITE	ACTION	TOTAL

TIME INVESTMENT	20 minutes	20 minutes	40 minutes
OBJECTIVE	PRACTICING PURPOSE		
BUILDING BLOCKS	Purpose, Focus/Control, Mind-Set, Standing on the Shoulders of Giants		
INSTRUCTIONS	Complete Exercise #8: Meditate on Mortality		

DAY 23

	RESEARCH	TOTAL

TIME INVESTMENT	60+ minutes	60+ minutes
OBJECTIVE	STANDING ON THE SHOULDERS OF GIANTS	
BUILDING BLOCKS	Purpose, Focus/Control, Mind-Set, Standing on the Shoulders of Giants	
INSTRUCTIONS	Complete Exercise #10: Stories of People You Admire	

DAY 24

	RESEARCH	WRITING	TOTAL

TIME INVESTMENT	30 minutes	20 minutes	50 minutes
OBJECTIVE	STANDING ON THE SHOULDERS OF GIANTS		
BUILDING BLOCKS	Purpose, Focus/Control, Mind-Set, Standing on the Shoulders of Giants		
INSTRUCTIONS	Complete Exercise #9: Understanding Family Stories		

NOTE: *This exercise can take time. To keep on target for this daily challenge, do parts (a) and (b) of the exercise. Take the time to pick the family member you want to research, and do thirty minutes of initial research. If you hit a wall, move on.*

DAY 25 TOTAL

TIME INVESTMENT	60 minutes	60 minutes
OBJECTIVE	BECOMING "COOL"	
BUILDING BLOCKS	Be Cool, Process, Mind-Set	
INSTRUCTIONS	Complete Exercise #11: Creating a Preparation Plan	

DAY 26 BREATHING TOTAL

TIME INVESTMENT	10 minutes	10 minutes
OBJECTIVE	BECOMING "COOL"	
BUILDING BLOCKS	Be Cool, Process, Mind-Set	
INSTRUCTIONS	Complete Exercise #12: Breathing	
	NOTE: *This exercise Ideally, one works to make this a complete habit on its own. Try it for the day as part of the holistic adversity training.*	

DAY 27 WATCH TOTAL

TIME INVESTMENT	10 minutes	10 minutes
OBJECTIVE	UNDERSTANDING GRATITUDE	
BUILDING BLOCKS	Gratitude, Mind-Set	
INSTRUCTIONS	Watch this TED talk by Louie Schwartzberg, it's brilliant: thegameofadversity.com/louie	

DAY 28 WRITE TOTAL

TIME INVESTMENT	45 minutes	45 minutes
OBJECTIVE	GRATITUDE	
BUILDING BLOCKS	Be Cool, Process, Mind-Set	
INSTRUCTIONS	Complete Exercise #14: The Gratitude Test. In the interest of time, do everything except driving to the person's house.	

DAY 29 BREATHING TOTAL

TIME INVESTMENT	10 minutes	10 minutes
OBJECTIVE	GRATITUDE	
BUILDING BLOCKS	Gratitude, Standing on the Shoulders of Giants, Mind-Set	
INSTRUCTIONS	Complete Exercise #15, Part 1: Thank You	

DAY 30 WRITE TOTAL

TIME INVESTMENT	60 minutes	60 minutes
OBJECTIVE	POSTMORTEM	
BUILDING BLOCKS	All	
INSTRUCTIONS	Write a 300–500 word piece on your experience of the thirty-day adversity challenge. How did it feel to work on these building blocks? What improvements have you made? What will you do tomorrow to build on these?	

If you've reached these words, then I assume you've made it. CONGRATULATIONS! You should be proud. Most people who read this book won't complete this challenge.

But this is only the beginning. You've committed yourself to understanding how adversity can be an opportunity. Like any set of skills, it takes discipline and effort to build and maintain your adversity muscles.

For me, it continues to be a worthwhile investment with evergreen rewards.

Thank you for investing your time in this book. I hope it provides you with the right blend of inspiration, foundation, and tactics to become better at whatever you work toward.

ACKNOWLEDGMENTS

I literally stand on the shoulders of giants. And I am grateful. This book would not have been a reality without the countless family, friends, mentors, and supporting cast who continue to influence me. **Thank you** to everyone who plays a main part or supporting role or who has just passed through the set for a day in this life of mine.

To Dad, thank you for teaching me how to be a man: to shake hands, to look people in the eye, and to respect my elders. Through your actions, you taught me to dream, question authority, be insatiably curious, and be a lifelong learner. I'm thankful for our friendship as I grew older. I miss you every day, and I love you. Consider this book to be an imaginary beer together.

To Mom, thank you for your persistence and empathy. Sometimes you don't know how strong you can be. Watching you overcome adversity in your life has been an integral part of shaping my mind-set. Love you, Mom.

To my grandfathers (Pop Pop and Grandpa), thank you for giving our family the opportunity to become a part of the middle class. You took bullets for us, traveled hundreds of miles by train to attend college while taking care of dying parents, and set the tone for your kids and grandkids to live lives and pursue dreams that you couldn't. I intend to carry on the torch. I don't take this responsibility lightly. I am proud of it. I love you and miss you.

To my wife, Sarah, thank you for dealing with this crazy husband of yours. You are the reason I want to get better every day. You keep me from falling apart. You roll your eyes at my crazy ideas and my even crazier actions. I need that! Thanks for understanding that the craziness is part of what makes me feel alive inside. It pushes me to move forward and to get up every morning. I love you, sweetie.

To Jesse, by the time this book is published, you'll be in Oakland, CA. Thank you for being you. I've learned so much from you. In many ways, I strive for the life you live: one of simplicity, freedom, and art. Thanks for keeping me sane and for continuing to strive for a purpose greater than yourself. You'll get there. I'm proud of you in every way. Love you, man.

To Uncle Doug and the DiNardo clan, thanks for your mentorship. Thanks for challenging me, asking questions, and listening to my long responses.

To Auntie Kerry, Aaron, and Sarah, I love you, and I hope this book serves an example of what we can all accomplish. I appreciate your love and support. Love you guys.

To Zach Obront, Tucker Max, Mohnish Soundararajan and Andrew Lynch—thank you for helping to make this idea into a reality. Your collaboration, professionalism, and expertise continue to drive me to become better. I am excited to see what is next for us.

It is often said that the best mentors are the ones who don't even know it. Special thanks to Tim Ferriss, Ryan Holiday, Lewis Howes, Martin Seligman, Steven Kotler, Mihaly Csikszentmihalyi, Elon Musk, Richard Branson, Peter Diomandis, Jerry Michalski, and Robbie Vitrano. Thank you for the work you do. You've influenced me to think deeper, act smarter, and work harder to be a positive influence in this world. I hope this book is one step in the right direction.

By all means, this is not an exhaustive list. I truly appreciate everyone who continues to support me and my work.

Cheers to working on what moves you.

Nick DiNardo is an entrepreneur, consultant and public speaker focused on adversity, personal growth and education. Throughout his career he has interviewed hundreds of experts on overcoming adversity, dealing with trauma and stress, and the crucial role that this plays in our cognitive development and education.

Nick has dealt with adversity his entire life. After his parents separated when he was seven years old, Nick went from living the American Dream to sleeping on the floor of a one room apartment and sharing a kitchen with 17 people. He managed to earn a football scholarship to Wesleyan University (CT) and ruptured the tendons in his knee in his senior year. He has started multiple companies, most of which failed. Time and time again he faced adversity—and continued to grow as a result. It is these lessons that led Nick to write The Game of Adversity, which distills cutting-edge psychological research as well as wisdom from Seneca, Viktor Frankl and Vince Lombardi, and turns it into actionable advice.

Nick is the producer and host of two podcasts: the Meet Education Project and the Sweet Adversity Podcast. He writes more about adversity and personal growth at NickDiNardo. com. He lives in North Attleboro, Massachusetts, with his wife Sarah.

40939288R00067

Made in the USA
Middletown, DE
27 February 2017